STRESS IN YOUR LIFE

A complete stress-reduction programme

– pinpoint your individual stressors
– learn a powerful relaxation technique
– tackle work-related stress
– free your energies to live your life more creatively

GW00713161

STRESS
IN YOUR LIFE

Stress affects us all to some extent. This new and individual approach to tackling stress is based upon a personal programme to promote relaxation and reduction of stress arousal.

KEN POWELL

THORSONS PUBLISHERS LIMITED
Wellingborough, Northamptonshire

First published 1988

British Library Cataloguing in Publication Data

Powell, Ken, *1929-*
   Stress in your life
   1. Stress (Psychology)   2. Stress
   (Physiology)   3. Self-care, Health
   I. Title
   158.1   BF575.S75

   ISBN 0–7225–1421–2

Published by Thorsons Publishers Limited,
Wellingborough, Northamptonshire, NN8 2RQ,
England

Printed in Great Britain by Richard Clay
Limited, Chichester, Sussex.

10 9 8 7 6 5 4 3 2 1

Contents

To Barbara

Preface

This book is about stress in your life. The word 'your' is important, because that is where the book focuses – on *you* personally. It is different from any other book you're likely to read on stress.

Stress results from the way you see potentially threatening events which you feel inadequate to cope with. These trigger an immediate physiological response in your body. You prepare to fight back, to flee or sometimes freeze in impotent inaction. You cannot deal effectively with the situation which confronts you.

Stress also has long-term effects: suppressed endorphines (you feel pain more often and more severely), weakened immune system (you become ill more frequently), there are adverse changes in your heart condition – plus many more health problems.

To tackle stress in your life, exact, specific and personal causes need to be pinpointed. Generalizations are insufficient. You need also to examine how individual stressors are part of larger and more powerful patterns.

This book works with you to help you uncover the meanings behind situations which stress you. Specifically designed techniques are provided which assist you to get to the heart of your problem and enable you to release energies to get on with the rest of your life.

This book also includes a powerful but completely safe relaxation technique which will reduce the harmful physiological effects which are part of the stress response. There is also a cassette you can purchase from the publishers or bookshops for you to use as you work through exercises which begin to reveal how you fashion your world.

The methods have been used by hundreds of managers, professionals and individuals in the United Kingdom, The Netherlands and other countries. They are now available to you.

The techniques are broadly within the framework of Personal Construct Psychology – a psychology concerned with the individual and his and her meaning of the world. It is at this level that we work together, tackling the problems of stress in your life.

This book is best not merely read but worked through. As some readers will skip parts that do not apply to them, instructions have been repeated. This may seem tedious but it is deliberate to save you having to refer back to earlier sections.

The key concept is to help you create control over your life and the way you live.

PART ONE

STRESS IN YOUR LIFE

CHAPTER 1

Introduction

'Monday is the sort of day you want to get over quickly', thought Frank as he slowly made his way down the long corridor to Bill Harris's office. Frank was almost unaware of the dull November clouds darkening the rain spattered windows as he vaguely wondered what Bill wanted. He'd worked with Bill ('with' he'd say, not 'for') now for over twelve years.

Frank took his time. He felt comfortable and easy. He knew his way around. Most of the hundred or so employees knew Frank. Eighteen years with a company and you do things smoothly, slowly and without too much conscious effort.

The office clock showed ten-thirty. Another normal day is what Frank expected as he opened the door and walked over to greet his boss.

Bill Harris, his manager, knew otherwise. He had to tell Frank that...

STOP READING NOW!

What for you would be the most stressful thing Bill could tell Frank?

Put this book down. Spend a moment or two considering what it might be that will stress Frank so much. Let the scene work through your imagination until you savour the feeling of the situation. Try to capture it fully until you almost feel it yourself.

You might have thought that the most stressful thing Frank could hear would be:

— 'you've been made redundant'
— 'you've been demoted'
— 'you've made a serious error'
— 'your wife has just been killed in an accident'.

You may have thought of something different. Or perhaps you couldn't think of anything. Such ideas do not come easily or comfortably into our minds. We find them too threatening. But many of us, by just mentally visualizing this five minute scene, will be able to share something of Frank's distress.

In fact, Frank is amazed how calm he felt.

'It is almost as if it is happening to someone else', he thought at the time.

Two days later the shock hit him.

What came into your mind about what might have stressed Frank, reflects something of what is likely to stress you. Hundreds of other readers will respond differently.

Let's look, for a moment, into your world and how certain events or situations might stress you. Go back to the last time you felt stressed. What was happening? What took place just before the stress incident? Now return to the actual stress-inducing situation. Where were you? Recapture the colours, time, physical appearance, even the smells of the place. Who was there? How did you physically feel? What did you do?

Give that incident a name. Something you can easily recall it by.

Now move to a scene which was pleasant. Perhaps your holiday, or a time you were rewarded for doing so well. Maybe it was a time when you were alone, walking through a shady, green valley on a warm summer's day, feeling free from all care.

Trust your own imagination to select *your* suitable situation or scene. Again recapture it in all aspects – even how you felt when you moved around, the sun on your face, the vivid colours of the sun-lit corn and the changing patterns as the breeze smoothed and ruffled the corn in the meadows.

Stay with your scene for a moment. Get the feel of it.

Notice how different physically you felt when you remembered the first episode and how you feel now. Even the memory of events such as these affects you physiologically.

Label this event as well as the earlier one by giving it a name.

Now select another event that stressed you. Think back over the last six months. What has come into your mind? Stay with whatever memory has surfaced. Elaborate it. Again capture the feel of it.

Name this event as you have done for the two earlier ones.

Write down each name, one underneath the other. Here's an example:

1 Told off by the boss.
2 Walking on the hills.
3 Row with husband/wife over holidays.

These remembered episodes in your life will help us look into your mind to see what it is that causes you stress. They provide you with a means of pinpointing some of the stressors in your life. You will see that it is not events themselves so much which harm you, but the meaning behind them.

Take your first event and the last one (that is, the two stressful events) and think of some common ways in which they go together. Do not just say that both stressed you, or something superficial like one and three happened on a Tuesday. Look for a quality or meaning which links them together. You may have to spend some minutes pondering over this. On the other hand you could have found that an idea flashed into your mind.

You might come up with something such as:

felt out of control
or
couldn't express my anger
or
felt I was a failure
or
felt rejected.

Your word or phrase may be quite different. Stay with what your mind has suggested — even if it seems a bit strange.

Now write down what you feel is the opposite to your words. Don't bother with dictionary meanings. Trust yourself to give what you feel is your opposite.

Here are some examples:

felt out of control ←→ could control events
couldn't express anger ←→ able to express feelings without being guilty
failure ←→ others see me as a success
rejected ←→ accepted

Whatever you have written is an important part of your mental world. Certainly only a small part but a part which in some way is connected with stress in your life. If the same events had happened and you had felt in control, then that event would not have been stressful. Stress is more in the meaning the event has for you, than in the event itself.

In the first example, stress seems to be

related to not being in control. It isn't the incident itself that causes problems but the feeling of not being able to control what happens. We might, in reality, be able to control the situation but if we believe that we cannot, then we act within our beliefs. We are then without power. Consider the implication of what this means. Think of how the same event might have been seen quite differently by someone else and because of this, experienced without stress.

In the second example stress seems to be connected with not being able to express emotions without feeling guilty.

The third one is around the area of being seen as a success, not necessarily success itself but being *seen* as successful.

Move away from these examples back to your own. Whatever words or phrases you came up with, trace back other incidents which recapture some of the same feelings.

Write these down. What is the common thread which links these incidents in your life? Are there many of them? Are they connected with work or with home? Or perhaps the relationship between the two? How did you attempt to cope?

What you have done is to capture some common factors or themes which cause stress in your life. It is these meanings you see or construct into situations which are the problem.

Other people might not feel stressed in identical circumstances because they see them differently. They do not read into the situations the negative aspects that you do. To take the examples mentioned earlier, some of us do not feel guilty about expressing our feelings.

Take the third example about failure. We might perceive criticisms by our boss as a problem-solving or learning exercise. When we fail at something, some of us do not see ourselves as failures only that we did not do a particular thing as well as it

could have been done. We try to make sure that we do not repeat the same mistake again. The error may have been important or quite unimportant. Others of us, out of the same material, turn ourselves into failures. The whole concept of 'failure' has different meanings. One meaning leads to a constructive, problem-solving approach, the other an almost total condemnation of our personality.

What this means is that, firstly, events which stress you may not stress others; therefore to tackle stress in *your* life, you need to pinpoint your personal stressors.

Secondly, it is not the event so much but the meaning you construct into the event which matters. It wasn't your boss's behaviour, it was the way you felt about being a 'failure', or how you couldn't express how you felt. You are likely to have felt physically unwell as you stood helpless before this (to you) all powerful figure. You kept the feeling tightly bottled up inside you. You took it home with you, carrying around a mass of unexpressed anger.

People react to stress in different physical ways. Some of us are head people: our eyes throb, our heads ache, our jaws stiffen. Others are neck or shoulder people. This is where we feel our pain. Some are back people, others suffer from stomach upsets. The stress stays with us physically as well as mentally.

The next important aspect is the way different meanings, triggering the stress response, link together to form larger patterns. These patterns are 'meta-meanings'. In some people stress is connected to one major meaning which is inherent in all stress situations. In others there are clusters of meanings and for some stress-meanings do not link together at all – many different factors are at work.

To tackle stress effectively, you need

not only to establish meanings behind stress events but also the way they are linked together. If they are all connected and you deal with the meta-meaning, you work at a level which releases stress from nearly all aspects of your life. The rest of us fight our battles on many fronts.

If people perceive the same event differently, then it must be that we could also develop alternative perceptions. Remember the comments about failure, about emotions, about criticisms. There are alternative meanings given to identical situations.

This provides a clue about how you could tackle stress in your life. By looking at events and their meanings (which might be hidden), we might start to consider alternative ways of perceiving things. These analyses might help release energies to deal with situations more constructively. If you don't feel a failure, you can actually learn from mistakes and become even more effective. If you feel that you can control events, you seek out ways in which you can do so. When you feel it is OK to express your feelings, then this is what you do and at least the other party knows how you feel. Of course, you may think it is inappropriate to do so but you do have the choice. You are not forced to remain dumb.

Another important aspect in reducing stress in your life is to be able to counteract the physical symptoms which accompany stress. Instead of being uptight, you feel relaxed but alert; in place of a general state of tension, you experience ease and peace in your life.

Let's look a bit more deeply at some research findings about stress. Many events have been suggested as contributing to stress in people. These include:

— adverse life events such as death of your spouse, an accident to you or someone close to you

— not really knowing what's expected of you

— work overload; just too much work, that's too complex and too little time to do it in

— lack of control; you respond to orders about what you do, how you do it and when. You do this daily for every minute of every work day, two hundred of them each year. You become alienated from your true self as you are relegated as if you were a small cog in a machine you hardly comprehend.

All these factors have been shown in research projects to be connected with stress, but when you look at people who say they are stressed, the answers are not so straightforward. Although research compares averages of groups who have control with those who do not, those who feel uncertain about their responsibilities with groups who do not and so on, there are differences *within* each group. Whilst the average suggests stress, some of those within the 'stressed' group feel OK, others are seriously stressed. The variability is considerable.

The trouble with averages is that they tend to smooth over differences. It is as if an average sized suit was made for everybody in the country. It might fit quite a few, but many would find it too large, or small, too wide or too narrow. Your stress might reflect averages obtained by researchers but it is likely that your stressors are a complex mixture. To help overcome stress in your life, you need to discover this complex pattern and work at your personal and individual level.

Let's look at some examples. For Joe it was the thought that at ten-past-two tomorrow afternoon he would have to walk in, stand up and present to his clients new proposals about the revised production control system. Joe sits and tries to outline what to say and what visual aids to use. He stares at a blank piece of paper. He writes the title, crosses it out, starts to make notes and then finds himself day dreaming about his last holiday. With a jerk, he pulls himself together and tries to return to his talk. He knows the scheme is good, in fact it is first rate, but he can't concentrate. He keeps thinking of tomorrow. He notices that his heart is pounding, his stomach feels uncomfortable and he's actually shaking. He feels sick, trapped and his feelings interfere with his thoughts. He can't prepare. But he must.

Mary has identical symptoms. But her problem is that she is out of milk and this means going to the shops – actually getting up, going out, walking half a mile, passing people on the way and then going into a shop, picking up a bottle of milk and paying for it. Like Joe her thoughts frighten her. She physically shakes as she prepares to go out. It is not that she is a coward. In fact she is very brave because she does venture out despite her feelings.

Charlie is going to spend the next two weeks on vacation on one of the lesser known Greek islands. He's worked hard throughout the year and feels he's earned and needs his vacation. To get there he must fly. This he dreads. His symptoms are similar to Mary's and Joe's but he knows that he can spend most of the flying time in an alcoholic haze. What worries him is that he will have to wait until after take-off until first drinks are served.

Jean feels the same about her next work appraisal – although she knows and likes her boss. She is also certain that she's doing a good job. But she hates the thought of it.

Tom shares similar feelings, only they are more frequent. He is a teacher and dreads every day having to work with his class. He lives from one vacation to the next.

And so it goes on. Stress-inducing incidents which are individual and personal. For some it is teaching, shopping, flying, working and meeting the challenge of making a presentation. Others *like* teaching, shopping, flying or making presentations.

What is being responded to is not so much the event itself but the meaning each of our characters has given to it

We all differ. What is challenge to one, terrifies another. There is a further way in which we differ and that is the way we respond to what we perceive. Even if you share an identical perception with someone, you may react more intensely or less so. In an emergency some of us respond calmly and tackle what needs to be done. The rest of us panic.

Research on stress usually aims to establish what situations and events make the average person feel anxious. Statistical analyses compare similarities or differences between averages. When results are significant – when they have a one in twenty or one in a hundred possibility of not being caused by chance – they are considered to indicate a stressor. Some examples have been given above: death of a partner, divorce, starting a new job and so on.

One famous study allocates points to potential stressful events. You add up these points and reach danger level if you score 150.

But as we have seen, life for each of us is different. Shopping does not appear on the list and yet for Mary this is the most threatening thing in her life. Holidays are the least threatening on the list – but for Charlie, if they include travelling by air, they represent his greatest fear.

To sum up – we have seen stress so far as consisting of:

1 An event or situation; this can be in the past, present or anticipated. It can be

real or imagined, recurring or one-off.

2 Our perception of that event or situation in which we see some form of threat.

3 The way we emotionally and physiologically respond to that perception.

4 The behaviour we employ to deal with our perceived threat.

In real life these aspects are not so neatly separated but it is convenient to divide them in this way so that we can consider each in turn. They also interact with each other. For example we are aware of our feelings and we note our behaviour. This then also becomes something we have to deal with. The fear of fear or the worry about being worried become stressful events in themselves. We are in a vicious circle with stress feeding us more stress.

Some of us generalize from one stress inducing situation to others which are similar in some way. More and more related situations stress us. We feel stressed in a tube train, then in a car, later in buses and eventually all travel affects us even to the stage where we feel we cannot leave our own home.

Stress is now disabling. We begin to see ourselves differently, redefining who we are – as a person who cannot cope. We play out that role. We begin to fear the feelings we get. More and more situations become threatening and they provide us with evidence that reinforces our view of ourselves. Yes, we feel, we were right when we thought we couldn't cope. The original cause of our problems no longer matters. Our anxiety seems to have a life of its own.

We also gain secondary advantages. Others feel sorry for us. They notice us and are kinder and more gentle to us. We may even get to like the attention we receive and this helps keep the behaviour going. At least we get care and attention. We are now somebody – different from the rest of them. We have a purpose in life – to survive.

This book will help you uncover the hidden meanings behind situations which stress you. It will assist you to link these meanings into larger patterns. Then instead of tackling events singly, you can work at a higher level, dealing with fundamental issues, freeing you to consider alternative ways of seeing things, releasing energies to help you fashion new creative strategies to tackle stress in your life.

This book is incomplete. It needs your help to finish it. Techniques are provided to help you examine your personal meanings. These are not enough. You have to *use* the techniques. If they remain on these pages, they can't help you. This is not the sort of book you read in the hope of finding some magic cure. You have to play your part. Sometimes it might be a bit painful. As you work through the exercises, however, you will gain an exciting insight into your personal world.

Additionally, you will learn a powerful but perfectly safe method of relaxation to reduce negative arousal which accompanies your stress. This you can use generally, so that daily you find yourself becoming more relaxed. You can also use it specifically in actual times of stress.

Let's return to Mary, Charlie and the others for a moment and see what is happening to them.

First there is an event which they construe in some way as threatening. This may be actual, imagined or anticipated.

Immediately, as soon as we recognize a stress situation, the sympathetic part of our autonomic nervous system is activated. This is an involuntary response. It just happens. (Although later you will learn some techniques which will help you control potential reaction to stress). Adrenaline (epinephrine) is released. Charlie and the rest of us are put on 'alert'. This stimulates the heart, causing it to beat more rapidly. Blood-pressure rises. Breathing quickens. Blood is redirected to the brain, heart and muscles. Cortisol is released; this thickens the blood so that it clots more easily. Hydrochloric acid in the stomach is increased. Digestion is slowed. There are changes in metabolism. The liver increases glucose in the blood.

If it is happening to you, you begin to notice that you sweat. You are aware of your pounding heart; your dry mouth. You may even feel sick. Like Charlie and the rest of them, you are now less able to deal with the stress-inducing event.

If you smoke, you excrete more nicotine (30 per cent compared with 6 per cent normally), so you inhale more or increase the number of cigarettes to maintain your nicotine level.

You are prepared for physical battle. When you hear the piercing sound of a nail over a piece of glass, you react strongly. This sound mimics the distress cry of certain primates, preparing them to flee or fight. So are you. Five thousand years ago this was useful. It helped us survive.

Sometimes the desire to run and fight are so strong and so equally balanced that all you can do is to freeze. Physically fighting, running away or becoming frozen into useless inaction don't help us deal with our boss or sort out relationship problems.

When our real, imagined or anticipated anxiety-producing event is over, the parasympathetic part of our autonomic nervous system takes over. Noradrenaline is released. We feel relaxed, relieved and at ease.

Immediate physiological responses to stress do not matter if they are infrequent. Some stress is even beneficial. We would be bored without it. It also helps get better results.

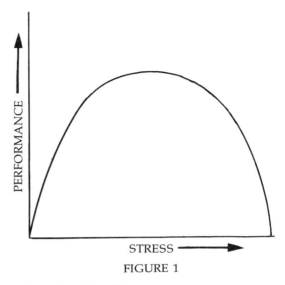

FIGURE 1

It works like this:

Without any stress we are lethargic and lack drive. As stress increases so too does our performance but it reaches a point where it begins to reduce our capacity to perform well.

Actors, musicians, public speakers and others need some tension to perform well. Too much is disastrous. They cannot think clearly or respond quickly; even freezing, being unable to do anything at all.

If stressful events are frequent we can still live a useful life. We are able to cope. But at a price. We do not enjoy life, we only get by. As one sufferer aptly put it: 'Life is an endurance test to be got over as quickly as possible'.

Our body adapts to the additional demands made on it. We learn coping strategies. But adaptation is finite – we can just hold out for so long.

Sooner or later we reach a breaking point. We experience burnout.

This is how it works:

The extra burden is just too much. During the coping phase, the repeated reactions to stress and later relief, as the situation passes, produce longer term physio-

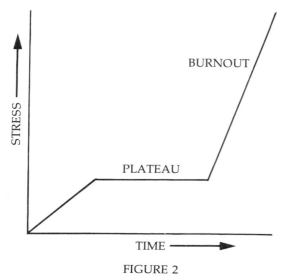

FIGURE 2

that stress is '...the physiological response ... involved in emotional or arousal reactions to threatening or unpleasant factors in life situations...' Lazarus and Launier describe it as a process in which perceived demands severely tax or exceed available coping resources. The word comes from Old English and is connected with distress.

Stress then is the frequent over-arousal in response to imagined, actual or anticipated situations which we construe as in some way threatening and which heavily tax or exceed our mental and physical resources to cope.

$$STRESS = arousal$$
$$+$$
$$meaning$$

The way out?

1 You need to look at the ways you personally construe (that is understand and perceive) situations which cause you stress. Your construing is the medium through which the objective outside world is translated into your inner reality. It is to this that you respond. You need to see how these form larger meanings and patterns.

2 When you have understood these patterns of stressors, you can re-examine them.

3 From this you can develop more effective strategies to tackle problems.

4 You can learn to reduce arousal both generally and specifically in stressful situations.

There is also an accompanying cassette which you can purchase to help you reduce harmful arousal more quickly.

Each of these steps will reduce stress in your life. Combined, they provide powerful benefits to help you move out of your depression, anxiety and fear into

logical problems. The hypothalamus in our brains has released ACTH as part of our stress response pattern and this has the side-effect of weakening our immune system, making us more vulnerable to viruses and bacteria. We become ill more frequently. Blood-pressure may not be permanently raised but the frequent surges begin to damage our heart. Frequent releases of noradrenaline constrict blood vessels, they can also alter the rhythm of our heartbeat.

During the coping stage we may even deny that we are stressed but friends notice that we are aggressive, irritable or apathetic. We smoke and drink more. We eat excessively. We exist but we do not live.

Seyle, who first used the term stress, described it as a 'non-specific response by the body to any demand made on it'. This can be severe or light, pleasant or unpleasant. This means that stress can be positive or negative. It is the negative aspects that we are concerned with. Some authorities confine the use of the word to its negative sense. Dr John Mason, one time president of the American Psychological Society, states a more constructive, meaningful and fulfilling world which you, yourself, will have created.

Many physical problems are likely to be helped by reducing stress. This does not mean that you should not consult your doctor. Problems can be caused by physical factors or have physical consequences as well as psychological ones. At a certain stage even psychologically induced illness needs medical attention. You need to check with your doctor.

Here are some problems – many of them physical – connected with stress:

feeling tired, even when you wake up
can't get to sleep, even though you feel exhausted
general anxiety and nervousness
high blood-pressure
frequent headaches
skin complaints
asthma
rheumatoid arthritis
depression
phobias
backache
stomach upsets

The notorious irritable bowel syndrome is a physical condition with no obvious physical cause. Stress seems to be implicated, according to a recent international symposium on the subject. Some with a different genetic make-up might develop high blood-pressure, others suffer in this way.

How will you know that you are stressed? The question hardly needs asking for those who are stressed. They know it. It is like asking somebody how they know that they are happy. They know. Some of the symptoms include: feeling unable to cope, worrying about the past and the future, having persistent negative thoughts, feeling restless and edgy, feeling a failure and lacking confidence, feeling anxious and apprehensive, having a

sense of dread about life, finding it difficult to concentrate and finish tasks. Sometimes the feeling is one of deadness and a lack of interest in anything.

For some stress is generated by behaviour which seeks challenge, is compulsively competitive, driving, task orientated, doing more than one job at a time, restless, over-committed. This is the typical so-called Type A personality which we will discuss later.

This is not one of those books that you can read, feel some mental uplift but which leaves your problem unsolved. You have to invest time and effort into working with it. Your stressors are likely to be complex. You need to pinpoint these.

Above all you have to start to take responsibility for your own life. You will not be handed a simple prescription. You will be given methods and a series of techniques which have helped others and can help you. Reducing stress frees you to become the sort of person you'd like to be, living in a way which suits your personality. You find satisfaction and fulfilment in daily living.

HOW THIS BOOK CAME ABOUT

After working with individuals and their stress and related problems for a number of years, I was asked to run seminars in industry to help managers and others tackle their work-related stress.

An initial investigation using repertory grids to examine how people perceive situations which they feel stress them, revealed that although there were common patterns of stressors which reflected other research, individual differences were considerable.

People differed in the situations which they saw as stressful. Some saw a particular reorganization as stimulating and rewarding, others saw it as a threat. They differed in the meanings they saw in identical situations and, even when the meanings are shared, the response varied. Some reacted intensely, others were much calmer.

The pattern of meanings was examined statistically (using principal component analysis of repertory grids). The structures which emerged from these analyses also differed considerably with some managers having all constructs (personal perceptions) leading to one major meaning which controlled a large part of their life. In others, there was no single common meaning. Stress had to be tackled on many fronts. For other people, there was a mixture of smaller clusters and separate constructs.

It seemed obvious that to work effectively stress would have to be tackled at an individual level. To have initiated organization changes would have missed key points for many people.

The initial work was repeated on similar and dissimilar groups – with the same results: events, meanings and the way perceptions were structured varied as far as stress was concerned.

This has proved to be the case with all subsequent groups.

The methods used were specially designed to elicit stress meanings. The versions in this book are the result of several modifications as they were used on 'stress' groups and on fellow professionals: clinical, educational and counselling psychologists and personnel managers and trainers.

The framework of the work is broadly within Personal Construct Psychology – a psychology concerned with the individual and his or her personal meaning.

TOPIC REFERENCES

Adverse life events and stress:
Rahe, R., *Life crisis and health changes*, Report 674, US Navy Bureau of Medicine and Surgery, 1967.

Ambiguity and stress:
Kahn, R.L., *Organizational stress*, Wiley, 1964.

Overload and stress:
Marshall, J. and Copper C.L., *Coping with work stress*, Gower, 1981.

Control and stress:
Frankenhauser, M. Lundber, U. and Forsum, L., 'Response to an achievement situation characterized by high controlability', *Biological Psychology*, 10, 79–91, 1979

Stress and coping:
Seyle, H., *Stress without distress*, Signet Press, 1976.

Stress and physiological effects:
Frankenhauser, M., *Psychobiological aspects of life stress; Coping and health.* (Levine ed.) Plenum Press, 1980.

Lazarus, R. and Launier, R., 'Stress-related transactions between person and environment' in *Perspectives in interactional psychology.* (Pervin, L.A. and Lewis, M. eds.) Plenum Press, 1978.

Stress defined:
Seyle, H., *Stress and distress*, Signet, 1974.

CHAPTER 2

The philosophy behind this book

When you enter into your future as you do every minute of the day and night, you do so looking backwards. As the future turns into the present, your past experience guides you. This experience helps you anticipate what is likely to happen and how to handle it.

Think of what it would be like if you had to learn everything anew each time; how to tie your shoelaces, fry an egg, deal with an awkward customer, use a word processor and all the other things you are able to do almost without thinking most of the time. Life would be impossible.

Consider for a moment some of the millions of skills and abilities you have... from telling the time to driving a car. And of the experiences which help you deal with social situations, solve problems and play your favourite sport. You could hardly live if you did not have these skills ready to use to help you as you move second by second into your future life. Whatever happens you have at least some capacity to deal with it.

This store of experience of yours is a massive and complex network of inter-related constructs. A construct may be thought of as one unit of a way of seeing or knowing about a part of the external world. Constructs are not static entities, they are processes. Sometimes they change drastically. Events may replicate previous happenings but often there are differences. A new situation may resemble an old one but there may be important variations.

These differences cause us to elaborate and modify our constructs and our construct system. If we still thought as we did as a child, we would not be able to tackle many of our adult responsibilities. We increase and modify our skills and understanding. We discard old ideas as they no longer fit our world. In a way we are like scientists, testing out how our ideas and knowledge fit our unfolding life.

From experience we develop hypotheses about how things are likely to be. When these things happen, our hypotheses are tested. We may have been right and this confirms that a particular set of constructs is valid for whatever situation we tested them on. Or they do not fit and we discard, or more usually, amend them. In this way our understanding grows.

It is impossible to grasp the ultimate reality of what the world is like. Even within the whole of our lifetime, we only contact a small part of it. So what we have to do is to construct a view of the world (which we hope has some relationship with reality), that helps us live, with competence and satisfaction. As the world changes and as we widen our experiences, we modify our construct system or some of the individual constructs contained within it.

The way you see things can vary from

the way others see the same situation. How do you think your little son sees his home? What about the newcomer in your office, how does she see the set up there? Can you go back to your first day in your job? How did everything look then? Or your first day at school? Remember that last meeting in your company, what would it be like to have been one of the other participants? How would they describe events; how would they depict your behaviour? If you were to discuss it, you might argue and fight about how things were. Yet is was the same meeting, the words were identical, so were the furniture, lighting and participants. Imagine others going back to their office, telling colleagues about the decisions made, colouring them to fit their own perceptions. Or perhaps you are colouring them?

Some of us are pessimists, others are more optimistic about events. Ask a pessimist to visit the local High Street and report on impressions. He talks of a drab day, dark clouds, how people look worn out, the intrusive noise of traffic, the crush of people in the supermarket and how the concert was half-empty.

The optimist will report a different picture. She will talk of the bustle of activity, the way people chat and laugh together, how children delight in jumping the rain puddles, and how easy it is to shop. Her concert is half-full!

The pessimist is validating his view of the world – that it is a pretty miserable place. So is the optimist. What she sees supports her way of viewing things.

In the Vietnam war, many soldiers who were wounded were overjoyed. They hardly noticed the pain of a missing hand, blown off by a hand-grenade. Their wounds meant an exit from the war. Someone else has a small cut on their left hand index finger. They are aware of the stinging all day. They com-

plain. Their work suffers. It seems to shut out all pleasure.

We fashion meanings from events, situations, objects and circumstances. Although there are external realities, our view of these is our own mental creation. The meaning is not so much intrinsically within the objects but imposed or fashioned by us out of external data.

We do this at a number of levels. Out of a mass of external stimuli, we are only equipped to receive a small part. If we are blind, colours, shapes, perspectives and form mean nothing to us. If we were a frog, all we would see would be contrasts, edges and fast moving spots. Our dog hears high pitched notes. We don't.

Out of the stimuli we are capable of receiving, we can only process a limited amount – so we have to be selective. We filter. Our selection is motivated. It is not at random. We take in what is meaningful to us. If you are in a large hall at a party, talking to a few friends in one corner and someone at the other end of the room mentions your name, you turn to that person and listen to what is being said about you. The person who mentioned your name could have been placed in any part of the room but you would still have picked up your name out of the background noise. You must have been receiving at a low level of awareness nearly everything that was going on but only attending to what was interesting to you.

This continues at deeper and deeper levels. We construct meaning out of external data by not only filtering but by imposing our construction on events.

As soon as we understand this, we begin to realize that others may see the same situation differently. This leads us to consider that we, ourselves, could reconstrue events. If there are various ways of viewing things, this opens up opportunities to explore alternative meanings and what our life might be like if we acted in line with new perceptions.

We also update our constructs or understandings of the world as we test them to see whether they work effectively for us. The world changes and so does our view of it. Think of the problems of being stuck with constructs that don't fit a changed environment. We act as if things were as they were but they are not. There is an awkwardness about how we live. We do things and we don't get the results we expect. You see it sometimes in very simple ways: the car won't work but we continue to try to start and restart it – until the battery runs down. Well, it did work once! Sometimes we pretend something unpleasant is not there – in the hope that it will go away. We carry on in the old way, stuck safely (we think) with our old constructs.

That our way of seeing the world is tentative and not fixed can be positive, open and creative. It means (within limits) that we can examine situations and explore different meanings. These other meanings free us. We are no longer trapped. They provide the possibilities of alternative actions. Forget about trying to start the car, check the petrol! What would it be like if... we act *as if* it were so and see what the results are.

These ideas are influenced by the philosophy behind the work of George Kelly. Many of the techniques outlined later to help you examine your world and its stressors were developed from Kelly's Personal Construct Psychology. The ideas reflect my own interpretation of Kelly's work and from testing the specific ideas outlined in this book whilst working with hundreds of people on their stress problems.

Personal Construct Psychology operates from the orientation of the person. It is through the person that the world is viewed. These views fashion the way we feel, the way we act, and what we believe. To understand a person's behaviour, sadness, joy or stress, we have to get into the individual world of that person. We have to see it from their viewpoint. This is why this book sets out to work at your level. It will be *your* understanding that will be unveiled through the special techniques provided.

As humans, we do not just respond to stimuli as the behaviourists would have us believe. We react to the meaning we give to events which confront us. This understanding is more than just cognitive. It influences the way we feel and how we behave. We could almost say that feeling/behaviour/cognition are one; although it helps to differentiate between them to study individual characteristics.

If, in a given situation, we feel that we do not have any control, we act *as if* we are unable to influence events. We feel powerless. We don't bother to try. The result is that we get nowhere. We feel alienated. We become depressed. We are the victim of circumstances – because we have made it so. This does not mean the external events mean nothing. They have their influence – sometimes a strong one. But there are different ways of perceiving what's happening, of what action we could take and how we could tackle things.

Other people respond to us from the way they see us. This is partly because of the way we present ourselves to them. If I think people dislike me, I act as if they dislike me. I do not smile at them, my non-verbal communication indicates that I am defensive and wish to cut myself off. I do not appear likeable. They stop being friendly to me. I am now disliked. I feel I was right all along; my view of myself is validated.

I might act this way for many reasons – perhaps I do not believe that I am worthy of being liked and loved. I feel I am likely to be rejected – so I reject first. It saves me being rejected. I choose deprivation rather than losing something important to me. Clients have said to me: 'Who could love anyone like me, there is nothing good in me'. Sometimes this is because they have set themselves impossible responsibilities and as they are human, fail to meet them. Some say that they have violent feelings, that they are angry with those they care for, or that they make mistakes. They have set up an impossible life for themselves. Never to fail or ever feel angry is to live a life of frequent stress.

Our beliefs and those of others create social realities. If this is so then we should be able to reverse the process and fashion positive and more healthy 'realities'. We can re-examine meanings we give to our life and from this new understanding begin to make changes. One way out of depression need not be drugs or ECT but to look at how and why I fashion my world the way I do.

If there are more productive ways of perceiving circumstances, you might wonder why we keep seeing things in such unconstructive ways. The answer is: because of the benefits!

Yes, amazing as it seems, we get something out of keeping things as they are. Change is too threatening. Within our view of the world it is better to remain cut off from outside living in our small bed-sit, without friends, responsibilities or having to bother with doing anything. Our womb-like constricted world is safe. If the hurt is so much when we lose something important to us, a way out of the dilemma is to deny ourselves the right to it. In this way it can never be taken away from us. What we have never had, we can never lose.

We have the capacity to change things. We are not the victims of our biography as Freud suggests. Like scientists we can set up experiments and test things out. What we need is the courage to do so.

This idea of 'testing' is important. It frees us from working in a success/failure framework. What we do may not work out, but that applies to many scientific experiments. Trying things out and not getting positive results enables us to move to other potentially more successful areas. We change our hypotheses and test again. Thus our life grows. So do our skills in testing.

You might see here that we have re-examined the meaning of 'failure'. We do not play safe and attempt nothing at all because we might fail.

Often failures (so-called) are the pathway to success. If you can drive, can you remember what it was like before you could? Or more especially the early lessons. Recall your inexpert attempts at a three-point turn, or at reversing. Recollect your very first drive.

Go back even further and see if you can recapture what it was like before you could do 'grown up, joined-together writing'. You saw such writing with as much understanding as you now have for Arabic (unless you are an Arab). What about your first cake, your initial attempt to stay on a bike, or ride a horse? These early failures were the route to your eventual competence. Most other things you'd like to do need to be learned. Maybe not in the same obvious way, but nevertheless learned. And you have to be prepared for failures as you move to success.

The other point is time. Some of us learned quickly to ride a bike; some were much slower. Nearly all got there in the end. By comparing yourself with others, you begin to bring in lots of 'shoulds'. 'I should be better'. 'I should be quicker'. 'I should be able to...' Who says so? Take your time, move at your own pace.

Learning goes through a number of

phases. First is being aware of your incompetence. You know that you need to learn. You then need insight about what it is you need to learn. You then practise and often make mistakes. Finally you reach an integrative stage where you are competent and can even monitor your own performance and deal with the unexpected such as interruptions. In much learning there is an initial spurt of success and then a plateau, where we don't feel we are making much headway. If we stick it out, we do make progress.

Now, because we have the capacity to change the way we see things, this does not mean we always will. We may cling to old perceptions in a changed world. We may even force others to see things our way. Stories are told of redundant executives acting as if they still had the old job. Even their wives are not informed. These former managers take the same 'going to work' route each day. Some even refuse to reduce their spending.

This sort of thinking is a type of hostility. The world has to fit the way I see it. I know it is not like I say it is but I am going to live as if it is. Others must see it my way as well.

Such behaviour is destructive. Why do we keep it then? The reason again is that it is too threatening to change. We cling to what deep down we know is false and expect others to validate the façade we present to the world. We might even fool ourselves, but somewhere within us is the knowledge that things are not as we pretend they are.

We have talked about 'constructs'. Let's look at some of their qualities. The physical world consists of atoms and neutrons bound into chemical structures. This is one level or type of description. We could also describe the world in terms of tables, chairs, houses, dogs, cats, people, cars and so on. An architect notes shapes, colours, forms and physical and functional relationships. One description is not necessarily better than another. It depends on what we're trying to do.

To discuss our world, we need to cut up reality into 'chunks' – for example words, concepts and ideas. They are not reality itself, only our symbols for it.

We create labels and although they have symbolic correspondence with reality, they are artificial. The map is not the landscape. We could have used other concepts and labels and broken up reality in different ways. Some cultures have no time in their language. Their syntax does not include tenses. There is no past, present and future. How could there be if there is no time! They see a world in which time and space are one (somewhat like modern physics does). Their language has degrees of certainty. Other cultures have no nouns. Everything is a happening. If you think about it, they might have a point. Some primitive tribes count: one, two, three, lot. You may think they are pretty stupid, but if you are a hunter, what's the point in having more than three dead animals for a small group of people. Their constructs fit their world.

With social reality the subject is even more complex. At one level of analysis social reality is created by the way we see things, how others see the same set of circumstances and how we together negotiate a common working meaning. From this we fashion our actions. Of course, society plays a part by socializing us with broad ready-made meanings, but our own subjectivity is the medium through which we take in and fashion these external messages. The potential for varying is great.

Some ways of seeing things are more fruitful than others. An artist sees shape, form, colour, contrast, structure and hidden meanings in a landscape. We see only a dull mist and a few trees. The landscape is physically identical in both cases.

Neither set of labels is right and the other wrong. They are alternative ways of construing that part of the world. Some of our constructions are less effective because they are not as fulfilling, creative, interesting, rewarding or as useful as they could be.

One client of mine who was connected with politics had to attend many receptions. She hated these. She hated them because she saw them as forums of people who were there to judge and appraise her. She also felt she was obliged to attend. We decided to elaborate her meaning of these events more deeply. We did it by making the appraisal much more efficient. She was asked to imagine everyone with small cards marking her out of ten for appearance, personality and other qualities. We had them on training courses to improve their judgement. Eventually she began to laugh and see how ridiculous the idea was. She ended up by reconstruing these receptions as events she could go to if she wished and which consisted of unimportant and superficial rituals. The events did not change, only her perception of them.

Let's look even more deeply at the qualities of a construct. They are bi-polar, that is they consist of a quality and its opposite. You saw this in the introduction to this book when you looked at some of your constructs connnected with stress.

For example:

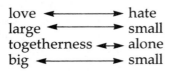

love ←——→ hate
large ←——→ small
togetherness ←→ alone
big ←——→ small

Sometimes one of the poles will be submerged, it is not available for us to use. A client who is depressed may not be able to see any opposite to depression. Constructs may be suspended because they have been repressed. Others are preverbal. We acquired them before we had language. We behave in accordance with some precept which we would find difficult to put into words. Such constructs still exert a powerful influence on our life.

Erik Erikson, a neo-Freudian psychologist, has suggested that within the first few weeks of life we acquire basic trust or mistrust. This emerges from our relationship with our mother. Whether this is as general or as black and white as Erikson suggests does not matter. It seems to apply to some people. At a very early age they learned to basically mistrust people. They are not aware that the person with whom they interact and relate is automatically being placed in the 'mistrust' category.

The two poles of your constructs may not correspond to dictionary definitions. One person on a management course I ran gave 'depression' as his opposite to 'challenge'. You might appreciate the implications of seeing work in this way.

Constructs are interlinked to other constructs to form complex systems and subsystems. Kelly called this concept the 'organizational corollary'. Some constructs within these systems are powerful and superordinate. Most powerful are core constructs. These include, for example, beliefs about the self, that is your own self-image. How you construe yourself is difficult to change.

Our construct system is hierarchical with higher level constructs 'governing' more subordinate but related ones. If you believe that you are no good as a person, you will think that others see you this way, you won't attempt difficult tasks, you might give up easily, you will constrict your life and avoid challenge. So for a seemingly small task, you will see yourself as incompetent.

Change, for a time, is easier for some behaviours at lower, subordinate levels, but powerful superordinate constructs force you back into your old habits. The change is only temporary.

I once had a client whose mouth was in a precancerous stage. She had been told that she had to give up smoking, otherwise, with almost complete certainty, she would get cancer of the mouth. She tried and failed. Her smoking was the only pleasure in her life. Take that away, and in her terms, she had nothing to live for.

Although our constructs are individual, personal to us, we do share some meanings with others. Our constructs have 'commonality'. We are on the same wavelength as others with whom we interact. Commonality aids social relationships. Without it, society would cease to function.

Some human interaction is still possible without commonality. We do not have to share the same constructs, but we do need to appreciate the meanings other people give to things. We can interact with them even if we cannot agree with them.

This quality was called 'sociality'. We construe the constructions of others. We can put ourselves in their shoes, seeing the world through their eyes, although we do not accept their viewpoint. Think of a mother who, to play with and care for her child, must be able to suspend her construct system (her adult viewpoint) to enter the world of her little child.

A dentist once told me that at about the age of three he 'saw' the stars for the first time. He appreciated their wonder and beauty. He was so taken up with this new image that he came home and wanted to share it with his parents. On the wall was an old and fairly valuable oil painting of a rural scene. He added stars to this by cutting them into the canvas. He felt he was giving something important to his family. His parents saw his act totally differently. He was told he was bad, evil and destruc-

tive. At that moment, he recalled, his world made no sense.

Consider the problems associated with trying to work with people where both sides are unable to get the feel of the construct systems of the other party — true discussion is impossible. Both are in different worlds. This applies to countries as they attempt to negotiate with each other.

More subtle, but equally a problem, is where both assume commonality. The words are identical but the meanings behind them differ. Both work on the assumption that they agree. In some work I have done with management and trade unions this is a major problem. 'Participation', 'industrial democracy', 'consultation' may be agreed as words but the meaning given by each side is quite different. Later each side cannot understand how the other can be so stupid, non-understanding and unco-operative when they have agreed objectives.

Where constructs are completely individualistic and not shared or understood by others, it is difficult or even impossible for interactions to take place. If others cannot see the way I see things, then discussion and negotiation are impossible.

I have adapted and used in industry one of Laing's methods of seeing the amount of correspondence between connected constructs of people working closely together.

Here are some of the questions for you to get the feel of what's behind our discussion so far. You answer the questions about somebody working for you, or you can modify the wording so that it fits a friend or partner.

You just tick the appropriate column. If you agree fully, your tick goes in box 1, if you totally disagree, it goes in box 5 etc.

The next stage is to complete a similar form as you feel your subordinate would

	FULLY			NOT AT ALL	
	1	2	3	4	5

I TRUST HIM/HER

I DELEGATE EFFECTIVELY TO HIM/HER

I COMMUNICATE EFFECTIVELY WITH HIM/HER

I AM OPEN AND HONEST WITH HIM/HER

I CONSULT WITH HIM/HER

I LET THEM PARTICIPATE IN DECISION MAKING

FIGURE 3

think you would fill it in. You may need to reread that statement, just a few times. You put yourself in the shoes of your subordinate and imagine him or her saying how he or she thinks you would fill it in.

Stage three is to complete a third form as you feel your subordinate would fill it in about you (you have to alter the questions slightly by changing the pronouns: 'I consult him/her' becomes 'My manager consults with me' and so on).

Your subordinate then completes a similar exercise about you. Place the forms on top of each other and hold them up to the light and you will see:

1 Commonality – you both agree.
2 Where you thought you agreed but you differ.
3 Where you both know there is disagreement.
4 Where you thought there was disagreement but in fact there is agreement.

This exercise is threatening. But it can lead to greater understanding. You might like to try this with your spouse or partner with different questions.

Where two people act as if both share common meanings and values but do not, the result is misunderstanding, miscommunication and frustration. If you know there is disagreement you can negotiate or agree to differ.

Here is another exercise for you to try: think of the last time you had a row with someone. Imagine that the person you had the row with is telling somebody else about it. What would they say?

How do you feel about the row now?

Now imagine your mother is talking about you. How would she describe you? What is your boss likely to say about you? And your neighbour? An ex-boy or girl friend?

What does it feel like to see yourself through the eyes of others?

Select an occasion that you enjoyed but your partner did not. Imagine your partner is describing what happened.

Think of a time when you felt really happy. Visualize this in your mind. See the place, the colours, how you moved around – even the smells. Now increase the brightness of the image. Double its size in your mind. Hold it and re-experience how you felt.

Consider an event which upset you. Again imagine it. Decrease the brightness of the image. Make it quite small and let it become fuzzy.

How do you feel about it now?

Think of yourself as an old person talking about some of the things which upset you this year.

Did you begin to feel differently about some of these events. Can you see how the same event can be viewed in different ways. As an old person, you probably felt that this year's disasters were of no consequence. You might feel that they were so minor, that when you are old you would not remember them at all.

Share some of your feelings with your partner. Look at things through his or her eyes. It is not that either you or your partner are right or wrong. Both viewpoints (and others) may be completely legitimate. Events can be perceived in many ways and feelings about them vary. It is OK to dislike things that other people like, as long as you allow them their preferences. What is destructive is to demand that others share your pet hates and delights.

This might bring you gently to the view that some of the situations in which you find yourself stressed can be seen in alternative ways and that some of the new ways of perceiving things may free you to act differently.

For example, in your work you may feel you have no power to change things. But power itself is a concept and if you see it one way, you can actually limit what you feel able to do. Power can be viewed from an elitist/Marxist stance: it is limited and fixed. If I take some power, you will lose some. So we fight over it. It becomes a win/lose situation.

Or you could see power as something that is created and not in limited supply. By banding together with others, you could create a power base. By working with so-called opponents, you might, together, produce solutions which meet the needs of all concerned; not 'my solution' or 'his solution' but 'our solution'.

If you see the construct of power as fixed, the only solutions are ones with winners and losers, or at best grey compromises. If you feel that 'they' are powerful and you are not, then you don't even try to change things. You just accept what you're given. When you believe that power can be created, you start to examine ways of changing things. You develop skills in persuasion, negotiation and communication.

Consider some of the skills you might start to acquire: how to define clearly what you want, why you want it, why you are asking for it at this time, why you have rejected alternatives and so on.

You learn to anticipate the counter arguments of your opponent. You acquire techniques which help you work out what you are going to do if you do not get what you want, rather than respond on the spur of the moment.

You become skilled in building in fail/safe methods to deal with vague promises so that if you get agreement, you know what to do if promises are not kept.

The important point here is that if you believe power is fixed and you do not have any, you do not start to help yourself to acquire these skills and techniques. You are not even in the race.

Considering alternatives frees you to develop creative solutions. You become proactive not just reacting to events. Kelly called this active fashioning of the circumstances 'aggression'. Results, of course, may be positive or harmful.

Stress and depression can be connected with the hopelessness of not feeling that you can do anything about situations. The way to cope is through acquiring the capacity to act effectively.

Let's look at some more qualities of

constructs. Constructs can be tight. This means that elements to which the constructs are applied are always seen in the same way. We see, for example, a person always at one end of the pole of a construct, he is a poor worker and that is that. At its extreme, we are almost obsessive. This is how things have to be.

Looseness is where we might apply one pole of a construct to an element one day and the other pole the next. We see a person as a good worker some days, and not so on other days. A tight construct makes prediction easy: we expect our worker to be a poor employee. We know where we are with him. With a loose construct, we don't know where we are; prediction is difficult. At the extreme this might apply to our total construct system; it may be so loose, in fact, that nothing hangs together.

Constructs and construct systems can be loosened and tightened. Both techniques are useful. Daydreaming, fantasy, free association, creativity, depend upon loose construing. We just let our thinking roam freely. A tight construct system may seem tidy but it ties us down. It may be consistent but consistently wrong! Loosening enables us to explore. But if we stop there, we have a mass of material, rich and stupid, interesting and useless, boring and outstanding, all mixed up together. We need to tighten things so that we get to grips with what might be useful. This then enables us to predict and test our predictions.

In Personal Construct Psychology, the creative cycle starts with loosening and ends with tightening. The process is a cycle with repeated loosening-tightening loops. Loose thinking leaves us with dreams, visions and ideas. Tightening takes some of these and helps us deal with reality.

Constructs can be constellatory. They govern other constructs. If a person is one thing then he is automatically a number of other things as well. We may see the good employee as always on time, having a tidy desk, dressing neatly, being polite and so on. People who are not like this are not good workers. Or the good mother is one who is always available for her children, keeps a neat home, is a good cook and always looks after her husband.

This is similar to stereotyping. A group of fixed qualities are bonded together. If a person is one thing, he is automatically other things as well. This is at its peak during a war. The enemy, every one of them, is seen as cruel, stupid and devious. Look how cartoons change. They graphically represent stereotyping. Examine old newspapers in museums; you can see how the French were represented when we were at war with them, how the Germans were later, and then the Russians.

This is a key part of racism. All people within a particular culture are held to have fixed negative qualities. I remember somebody telling me that they had employed a worker with a beard and he'd turned out totally unreliable, so no other person with a beard was to be employed in that company. From one example, generalizations had been made that included all people with beards as useless!

We can apply this to ourselves. If we fail at something we may start construing ourselves as a failure. A failure in one thing means a failure in all things – and we are generally no good, useless and so on. We play the role of a failure, expecting not to succeed and when we fail (as we will more often with that attitude of mind), the mistake confirms our view of ourselves.

Another example is that we might perceive a public school person as bright, intelligent, witty, sophisticated and worldly wise; whereas they will vary on all these and other qualities.

Another quality is called pre-emptive. Things, events or persons are seen in one way and only that way. The tight construct mentioned earlier about the poor worker was pre-emptive. Another example is to see someone as bloody-minded. That's all. Nothing else. No other qualities. The opposite is for constructs to be propositional or flexible. Our worker may be a poor time keeper but produces quality work, he is also friendly but doesn't always keep his promises.

Hostility has already been mentioned. It is our repeated efforts to prove – despite evidence to the contrary – that the way we see things is correct. This can apply at all levels from the scientist who defends his outdated theory to a widower who acts as if his wife is still alive and remains in a frozen half-life.

Guilt is where we are dislodged from our core structures. We act differently from the sort of person we believe we are. You have heard people say 'I wasn't myself when I did it'. We need not act 'immorally'. A thief in a family of thieves feels guilty if he co-operates with the police. We frequently feel stressed because we do not live up to self-imposed expectations about how we should be.

Anxiety is our awareness that we do not have the experience to cope with events which confront us. What is happening does not make much sense to us. We cannot get to grips with our immediate world.

Threat is the awareness that what we face might result in important changes in our core structures. We may need change so radically that we will become no longer the person we think we are.

Threat is a major component of stress. We see ourselves as people who should be able to cope with life and therefore we expect to handle the circumstances which confront us. Being unable to cope with

life means that we are no longer so sure of who we are. We do not fit the image we have of the sort of people we should be. We accept as legitimate the demands made on us. These may have been clearly spelled out to us or they may be more subtle. We obey rules that we are unaware of and therefore have never questioned. We also accept that we should be able to cope. We find that we cannot. It is all too much. We become stressed, only allowing ourselves a respite when we have a serious breakdown. This is, to us, the only socially acceptable way out.

From this, it follows that stress is a socially constructed disease. We accept the perceived demands made on us. We attempt to meet them despite hardship to ourselves. We move beyond what we can cope with and feel obliged to continue to do so until the stress is too much and feel only then that society will permit us to opt out.

We need to examine the demands we think are made of us. Have we got this right in the first place? Next we can consider our expectations about how far we should go in fulfilling such role demands at all times. We may find that they can be negotiated, that we are allowed to prioritize and sacrifice less important aspects of what needs to be done.

Fear is like a threat but not so much concerned with core structures. We may be afraid to visit our dentist but to feel so does not change ourselves radically.

Constriction is where we reduce our world to what is manageable. To remain in one room, eating, sleeping and passing our lives there is safe. We have made our life small enough so that we can cope with it. There are many less dramatic ways in which we constrict our world – we may never fly to our holiday destination (therefore we cannot visit far away places), we refuse to learn to drive, never change our job, won't risk getting married because we have to commit ourselves. Constriction gives us safety. The cost is lack of movement and growth.

There are times when constriction is effective. We have too much to handle so we limit ourselves to more important aspects. Sometimes it is too much for us and we need to desert.

The opposite to constriction is dilation, where we reorganize our construct system (or part of it) to a more comprehensive level.

Do not worry if you do not understand all these labels. The important point is for you to understand your construct system at least as far as stress is concerned and realize that constructs do not have to remain fixed.

To get the flavour of your mental world and some of its constructs, here is a small start with a technique called repertory grid. You will be using this technique later in much more detail to look at the stress patterns in your life.

This is where you stop reading this book and start examining your life! Take your time and work slowly.

There are six elements in this minigrid.

1 The first is yourself now.

2 The second is yourself as you would like to be.

3 The third is yourself as a small child.

4 The fourth is yourself as a stressed person.

5 The fifth is you as an unstressed person.

6 Finally someone you feel is successful.

Take the first three. Of these three, which two would you say are more alike. In what way are they more alike. Which is the odd one out?

There is no right answer, only your answer. Try not to select something superficial like 1 and 2 go together

because they are both the adult 'you'. Think about qualities that make them alike.

You may, for example, select 1 and 3 as being alike and two as the odd one out because 'vulnerable' comes into your mind as a quality that links them together.

When you've got your first quality (it is called a construct), think of its opposite. Do not stick to a dictionary opposite, give what you feel is right for you.

You may feel that your opposite to 'vulnerable' is 'powerful'.

Both 'vulnerable' and 'powerful' are part of one construct. They are at either ends of the pole of this construct:

vulnerable $\longleftrightarrow$ powerful

Already you have entered into your personal construct system – a small way in which you see your world.

In the example, 'vulnerable'$\longleftrightarrow$ powerful' are a way of construing the world. You could then apply this construct to the other elements:

Do remember that your way of putting two of the elements together is likely to be quite different from these examples. Trust yourself. Write down whatever comes into your mind.

Your next step is to apply your construct to all the other elements, for example:

stressed you .... vulnerable
unstressed you .... powerful
successful person .... powerful

Write your elements along the top of the grid form in figure 6 and your first construct in the first row. Figure 4 shows you how:

Now allocate points to how this first construct fits each of the elements.

Give 1 point if the left hand pole of the construct (in our example 'vulnerable') fits an element exactly.

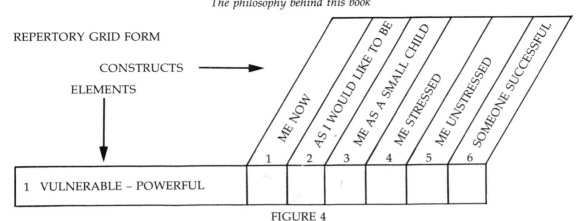

FIGURE 4

Allocate 2 points if it is in the middle and 3 points if it links with the right hand side of the construct ('powerful' in the example).

What you are doing is grading on a scale of 1 to 3 how well constructs fit each element.

Take a look at figure 5 to show you how it's done. Remember your gradings are likely to be different.

It is worth getting the hang of this exercise because it is the beginning of a powerful way of entering your mental world.

Place your numbers in the grid form in figure 6.

You might be able to see from the example that a successful person is seen as powerful and so is the self-like-to-be. Success seems to be linked to having power and so does the absence of stress. This person seems to see himself as powerless, stressful and vulnerable.

When you've done this, take the next three elements, numbers 4, 5 and 6:

4 self as a stressed person
5 self as an unstressed person
6 someone who is successful

Again select the two which you feel go together. When you've got this, ask yourself in what way do they go together; what is the quality that links them? Aim to get a different quality from the first one. This now is your second construct.

Work out what for you is its opposite

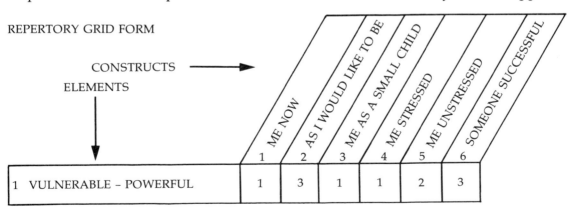

FIGURE 5

REPERTORY GRID FORM

CONSTRUCTS ⟶

ELEMENTS

		ME NOW	AS I WOULD LIKE TO BE	ME AS A SMALL CHILD	ME STRESSED	ME UNSTRESSED	SOMEONE SUCCESSFUL
		1	2	3	4	5	6
1	Vulnerable Powerful.	3	3	1	1	2	3
2	Static Movement.	2	3	1	1	2	3
3							
4							
5							
6							

FIGURE 6

and place both poles in the second row of the construct form in figure 6. Figure 7 is an example of what to do.

Again allocate numbers 1, 2 or 3 according to how you feel the construct fits each of the elements as has been done in figure 7.

You might select 4 and 6 as similar and feel that the construct which they share is 'drive'. Your opposite might be 'passive'. So in some way you see stress connected with drive.

In the example you might already begin to see a pattern emerging. Drive pro-

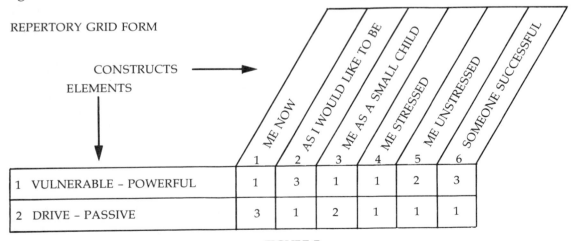

REPERTORY GRID FORM

CONSTRUCTS ⟶

ELEMENTS

		ME NOW	AS I WOULD LIKE TO BE	ME AS A SMALL CHILD	ME STRESSED	ME UNSTRESSED	SOMEONE SUCCESSFUL
		1	2	3	4	5	6
1	VULNERABLE – POWERFUL	1	3	1	1	2	3
2	DRIVE – PASSIVE	3	1	2	1	1	1

FIGURE 7

34

duces stress as well as success. Our friend wants to have more drive and to be more successful but he also wants less stress. You can see his dilemma. He feels that drive is necessary for success and that's what he wants. The problem is that (for him) drive also produces stress. That's what he doesn't want. He is trapped by wanting something which the means of achieving is a problem. He is going to suffer either way.

Your second construct may well be different. You may find a pattern, or you may not. Your constructs may pose a dilemma for you or they may be quite straightforward.

Continue in the same way with other combinations:

for your third construct take combinations – 1, 3 and 6

for your fourth construct take combinations – 2, 5 and 6

Each time selecting the two which go together and working out what it is that links them. Then decide on your opposite. Write both poles along the rows of the construct form in figure 6.

Allocate grading of the constructs to fit the elements and add them to your form. Your final combinations are:

1 2 5
2 3 6

This gives you six constructs and completes your form. You may find that you cannot get six. Do not worry, just use whatever number you can. You may even think of more than one construct from any one combination. If so include them.

Take a look at the differences in the numbers allocated to 'you now' and 'you as you would like to be'. Is it very great? If so what does it say about your life?

See what else you can read into your grid.

You may already have gained some insight into how parts of your world stress you. Do not worry if you do not understand all these ideas fully or remember them. You will find as you work through practical exercises about your own life they become clear. It is useful for you, however, at this stage to have some idea of the philosophy behind what you are going to do, to get a feel of what it is all about and begin some practice in the journey you are going to take into your personal world.

TOPIC REFERENCES

Adams-Weber, J. R., *Personal construct theory: concepts and applications*, Wiley, 1979.

Bannister, D. and Fransella, F., *Inquiring Man – The theory of personal constructs*, Penguin 1971.

Beail, N. (ed), *Repertory grid technique and personal construct psychology*, Croom Helm, 1985.

Social construction:
Berger, P.L. and Luckman, T., *The Social Construction of Reality*, Penguin, 1966.

Basic trust:
Erikson, Erik, *Childhood and society*, Paladin, 1977.

Repertory grid:
Fransella, F. and Bannister, D., *A manual for repertory grid techniques*. Academic Press, 1977.

Constructs and construct systems:
Kelly, G., *The psychology of personal constructs*, vols. 1 and 2. Norton, 1955.

Hostility:
Kelly, G., *The psychology of personal constructs*, vols. 1 and 2, Norton, 1955.

Organization, individual, commonality and sociality corollaries:

Kelly, G., *The psychology of personal constructs*, vols. 1 and 2. Norton, 1955.

Commonality test:

Laing, R. D., *The Divided Self*, Penguin, 1965.

Tightness, loosening, guilt, anxiety, constriction and dilation:

Kelly, G., *The psychology of personal constructs*.

CHAPTER 3

Pinpointing your stressors

Stress, as you have seen, is a complex combination of and interrelationships between:

1 Events, situations or circumstances – past, present or anticipated; actual or imagined.

2 The meaning seen in such events – containing some form of threat – hidden or overt.

3 Response to the meaning given to these events – a complex mixture of physiological factors which have immediate and long-term repercussions.

4 Behavioural response – this in turn becomes an event of which you are aware and is fed into the system and can further intensify stress as you realize that you are not coping as you feel you should.

Some of these events are in the past. They might be major life changes which are still causing problems in your present day living. Death of someone you loved, loss of a job, failing an important exam, moving home and finding that you do not like your new neighbourhood may still hurt months or even years later.

Stress may be connected with anticipated events. You fear the possible loss of your job, you think your loved one might desert you, the anticipated bankruptcy threatens or you feel at thirty that you may still be alone at forty.

Other stress is rooted firmly in present events. These may be major items or masses of smaller frustrations which repeat themselves daily.

The daily hassle of life can be particularly stressful: the car that won't start, losing things, or putting on weight. Kanner found 117 possible hassles which were more closely related to stress than major events.

Limited stress is beneficial, but sustained over a long period it leads to physical as well as psychological problems. Your blood-pressure may not be generally too high but frequent surges which flare up as part of your stress-response are harmful; your immune system is weakened, resulting in more frequent illnesses.

You become more sensitive to pain. Sleeping patterns are disrupted. You do not wake up refreshed. Stomach upsets are part of your life. You are irritable and difficult to live with. This causes extra problems for you to cope with. It is now even more difficult to tackle the causes of stress in your life. You enter a vicious circle and just about cope. One day there is an event too much. In itself it is not so threatening but on top of everything else, you find that you have reached your limit. You can cope no longer.

To get to grips with the problem, your first step is to pinpoint some of the stress-inducing circumstances in your life. You then need to examine the meaning behind such events. In the last chapter we called these perceptions 'constructs'. Stress is the result of your reaction to these constructs rather than a direct response to the circumstances themselves.

In the last chapter, you practised eliciting some of your own constructs. In this section, you will go deeper and also see how certain constructs cluster together to form meta-meanings. Working at this level enables you to tackle stress more powerfully as these meta-meanings 'control' lower level constructs.

Let's look at how the process has worked for others before you start on your own analysis. Ben was a manager whose problem was work overload (or so he thought). He tried to delegate some of his tasks and to reduce and reorganize others. Nothing seemed to work. He found that he could not prioritize. He always seemed overloaded. He found it more and more difficult to cope as his work problems meant that he couldn't sleep so well.

When Ben's problem was examined more deeply, Ben found that he was a perfectionist and second best was not good enough for him. Everything had to be perfect. To be perfect in an imperfect world is impossible. To select priorities meant that part of his work was not done fully or at all. Ben felt that he *had* to produce full results in all areas and all at high standard. His company wanted results of the more important tasks quickly. To work perfectly was too slow for them.

Ben was in a trap. He was pushed by his manager to get things done. If he succeeded, he could see the imperfections of his labours and he kept thinking of all the other items that needed attention. He tried to do two things at the same time and ended up in a muddle.

Once Ben established his inner need for perfection, he worked on why this was so important to him. He looked at the impossibility of trying to be perfect in an imperfect world. He examined how 'perfec-

tion' was less productive for his organization. He considered how his subordinates were not given responsible tasks and how he was, in effect, training second rate assistants because of the way he supervised them too closely. This exploration was painful. He felt physically hurt. His whole life had been based around trying to be perfect.

Ben began to trace back his idea of perfection. He found that it was a powerful message from his childhood. Both his parents had impressed upon him that this was how he was supposed to live his life. Forty years later, Ben was trying to live in an adult world under the guidance of out-dated childhood strictures.

It was not that Ben had to give up the idea of high quality completely but to learn to apply this only to important tasks that required such standards. Ben had begun to revise his construct system. He began to redefine what his job was about.

Previous attempts to reduce Ben's work load had failed. Once Ben had pinpointed the root of his problem (and it was deeper and more complex than the above sentences suggest), he saw things differently and this began to release energies that helped him become more creative and constructive.

To have cut Ben's work-load would have failed. To provide him with extra staff would have actually added to his problem rather than solved it. It was not the external tasks which were in the way. It was the way Ben saw things.

Take a quite different example. Terry's problems were all around going out meeting people. She was terrified of her 'panic attacks'. She also felt depersonalized at times, as if she was cut off from other people and her immediate environment. She said it was like having a mental wall around her. She felt that she was going out of her mind. Terry also felt completely depressed. Each day she would wake and feel as if there was a lead weight on her and that she had to get through the whole day.

Terry's programme was in layers. She first examined the meaning she gave to her depersonalization. This was completely negative. She then listed positive qualities it might perform. She came up with many: it made her feel safe as she was cut off from danger; it protected her; it warned her that she was attempting too much; it provided an excuse for her not to bother. She recalled that she did feel a sense of peace when this 'cloud' enveloped her. It some ways it seemed her friend.

This realization took away some of her fear.

She next looked at her panic attacks. Her major problem was fear of fear. In small doses at first, she faced some of the things that caused these attacks, being willing to accept her fear. By doing this she found it actually diminished.

Her depression lifted as she found she had some control over her life. Terry began to make slow progress.

Now it is your turn to work through your potential stressors. To do so, you will be using another repertory grid.

The exercises will take some time. You may wish to work over a number of sessions rather than just one long one. The exercises are well worth doing because they will present to you your world in the way you see it. You will be guided through step by step. Just take your time. Most people find the journey exciting, rewarding and meaningful once they have got the hang of what's necessary.

To start, you will need to select some actual events in your life which have stressed you. These events are called 'elements'.

To help you establish your elements, here is a series of questions. Write your answers on a separate sheet of paper. Try to think of one or two words which sum up and remind you of your answers to each question. This saves too much writing. Later you can transfer your answers to the repertory grid form provided.

STEP ONE

Answer these questions:

1 Think of a real event in your life in the last twelve months which has stressed you. (Frequently the best answer is the one which came into your mind straightaway). This might include such events as moving home, having a serious row with your neighbour, losing your job and so on.

2 Think of something fairly important which happened to you in the last twelve months which did not stress you. This might include getting promoted, passing an exam, taking up a new hobby etc.

3 Think of some other event in your life which has stressed you, or the most stressful activity in your life at present.

4 Imagine any sort of activity which would not stress you. This could be an actual pastime, hobby, job you've done or could imagine doing. This might include imagining taking up a sport such as skiing, taking a long vacation to the Far East or something that you actually do which is not adversely stressful.

5 Think of the worst thing that could realistically happen to you which would stress you. Most of us do not have any problems here in thinking of examples. This may be an anticipated event that you actually fear and has been worrying you for some time.

6 Think of a fairly routine activity which stresses or irritates you in some way. This can be anything from packing a suitcase to ironing clothes, parking the

car to cutting the grass. You can include here activities which occur from time to time and are part of your life. You might, for instance, include such activities as 'driving to work', 'chairing your community association meeting', 'trying to get your daughter to tidy her room' or whatever else applies to you personally.

7 Now think of a routine activity which does not stress you.

8 What is the last stress inducing event that comes into your mind or the previous one if you have already used this example?

9 Just think of any event that stands out in your life from the last month. This need not be connected with stress.

Do not worry if you cannot find nine elements, work with what you have got. If your life is very stressful and you find that you have more than one answer to any question, include the extra elements as well.

You should now have nine answers or elements. They represent events in your life, either actual (as in most questions), or imagined as in questions 4 and 5.

Here are the sort of answers that others have given:

1 Receiving a heavy income tax demand.

2 Going on a pleasant holiday.

3 Driving for many hours through a heavy storm.

4 Going for a long walk on a fine day.

5 Forgetting to turn up for an important appointment.

6 Packing before a trip.

7 Using a word processor.

8 Trying to get an urgent job done with insufficient time.

9 An argument in a shop over faulty goods.

Each of these was abbreviated:

1 Tax.

2 Holiday.
3 Driving.
4 Walking.
5 Forgetting.
6 Packing.
7 Word processor.
8 No time.
9 Argument.

Reread the questions and go through your answers again and change any that you wish.

STEP TWO

Write your elements (or their abbreviations) across the element column of the grid form:

STEP THREE

This is the most difficult step. You will need to do a lot of thinking. There is no right answer, only your answer. This is your first step in entering your personal world of stress.

Select elements 1, 2 and 3.

As you did with the exercise in the last chapter, ask yourself which two go together and which is the odd one out. Avoid anything that is superficial like two happened on a Monday and the other at the end of the week. Also do not say that two caused stress and the odd one out did not.

Here are some examples connected with the list above:

'felt could not cope, powerless, out of control', linking elements one and three together.

here's another: 'felt uncertain, didn't know what to do', again linking elements one and three

and another: 'failure'

These words that you have selected are called *constructs*. Constructs, as you have already read, represents ways in which you see the world. They are units of perception or meaning. Yours are likely

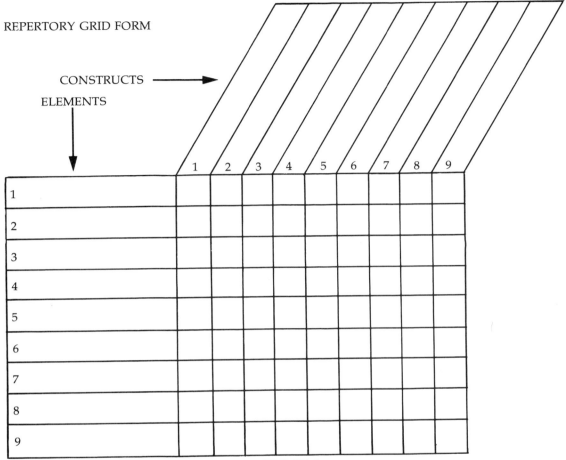

FIGURE 8

to differ from the examples. You need to trust yourself to work with what emerges from your own mind.

STEP FOUR

Now ask yourself what is *your* opposite to the first construct you have selected. This should be your opposite – not necessarily a dictionary one. Think about it, feel what it is all about and put down what comes into your mind.

Constructs consist of two ends or poles:

emergent end ◄─► the opposite

The emergent end is the one that you first thought of. It may be positive,

negative or indifferent. You then consider your opposite.

For example, here are some possible opposites for the examples given above:

felt unable to cope ◄────► in control
uncertainty ◄────► certainty
failure ◄────► certain of success
losing control ◄────► in control

These examples already provide some insight into meanings given to events which cause stress. Some of them are about not being in control, fear of failing or having to deal with uncertainty.

The important point is that the events in themselves do not intrinsically have

41

these qualities. Whilst for many of us receiving a heavy tax demand might be stressful, for others it might not. They may see it as confirmation of their worth, remind them of their large income; or leave it to their accountants to deal with; or feel anger at parting with such a large amount. Likewise some find using a word processor stressful others actually find it fun, the rest of us are indifferent, finding using it of no particular importance and certainly not especially stressful.

STEP FIVE

You need to pause here and consider the implications of the last paragraph. Events (elements) themselves are only raw data. It is the meaning you place on those events that triggers the stress response. There are many events which are stressful to some which others find relaxing or positive in their lives – for example horse riding, skiing, public speaking, parachute jumping, breeding rats and so on. There are other activities which many of us hardly notice but which are stressful to some people. These include shopping, going to parties, meeting new people, travelling in lifts etc.

Now relate these ideas to your own constructs. Are the external circumstances which induce a stress response in you likely to produce similar response in others? For some – yes; for others – no. Look at those people who handle such situations with ease.

When you consider the meaning you construct into your particular stressors, such as not being in control, having to deal with ambiguity or feeling that you might fail, then you join others who share your worries and concerns even if it is different events which cause their problems. Even here, however, not everyone who feels not in control or has to deal

with ambiguity etc becomes stressed. We all respond differently to what we perceive. In an emergency some of us panic, others react calmly. Some of us are happy to place control in the hands of others or we accept having to live in a world which cannot offer us any real certainty. There are persons who actually delight in uncertainty. For them it makes life more interesting.

We may share the same meaning from the same or different events and we may react to that meaning with similar or quite different intensity.

Although you have only started the exercise, you may find that suggestions are already emerging which will help reduce stress in your life. Make a note of these. Later you will find that you can work at a number of levels. For instance, if you feel overloaded at work, you can consider a number of options:

tackle the job itself by

1 Delegating.
2 Prioritizing.
3 Changing your job.
4 Finding out where the bottlenecks are and improving your skills in this area.
5 Pacing your work better.
6 Discussing with your manager how you could shed some of your tasks.
7 Automating part of the work.
8 Becoming more efficient in time management.
Or look outside the job by:
9 Developing compensatory interests.
10 Learning to relax.

You might be able to think of other possibilities.

Another and even more important way is to examine constructs connected with the job. For example, if your construct turns out to be connected with fear of failing, start to consider what failure means to you – why you have to be the sort of person who always has to succeed. You might also look at whether success/failure apply to all. When you look at your job more dispassionately, you may feel that some aspects do turn out well, some not too badly and some not as good as they could have been. These categories may be more useful ones than 'success/failure'. It could also be that what you see as 'failure' is not construed so by others. You could check with your manager. You might look at how impossible it is to be perfect at all times (remember Ben?).

You could work on ways to handle things differently, such as isolating key elements which cause most of the difficulties and concentrate on those.

If your problem is in the area of uncertainty, you could quantify uncertainty on a scale of 1–10, 10 being completely uncertain and 1 being quite certain. Note which level starts to bother you. It might be that at (your subjective evaluation of) 6 you begin to feel stressed. You could then not try to remove ambiguity but *reduce* it. You may find ways of changing 6 to 5.

Let's move on with the exercise so that you can delve more deeply into your mental world connected with stress.

STEP SIX

The next step is to enter your construct.

Note positive and opposite poles in the first construct row. To make it easier for yourself later, place the negative part of the construct (the stress producing one) on the left-hand side.

If you have been thinking about the implications of what has emerged for you, make some notes. You may find it helpful to keep a notebook containing your comments and ideas that you want to follow up later.

STEP SEVEN

For each element that has the same or similar quality to the left hand part of your construct, place a tick in the appropriate cell. Say you think elements numbers 1, 3, 5 and 7 are similar, tick these.

Now put a cross where you feel the opposite applies.

Where you feel that the construct is neither appropriate nor its opposite write in an 'O'.

You tick the elements which correspond to the left-hand pole of the construct, you mark those for which the opposite is more appropriate (they fit more with the right-hand side of the construct), with a cross and those in the middle or for which the construct does not fit at all

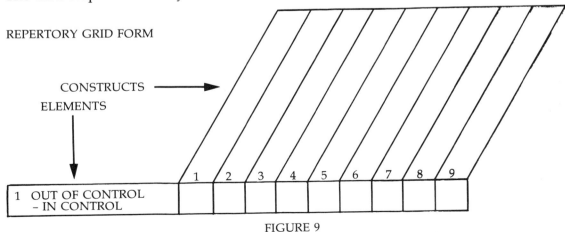

REPERTORY GRID FORM

CONSTRUCTS

ELEMENTS

1 OUT OF CONTROL
  – IN CONTROL

FIGURE 9

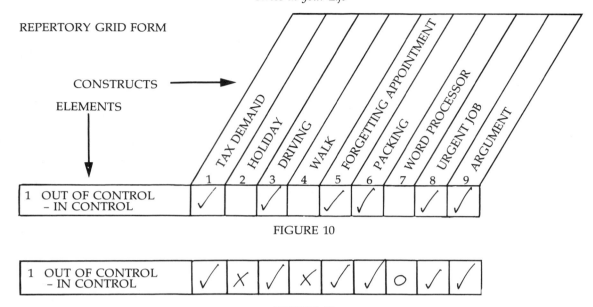

REPERTORY GRID FORM

CONSTRUCTS

ELEMENTS

	TAX DEMAND	HOLIDAY	DRIVING	WALK	FORGETTING APPOINTMENT	PACKING	WORD PROCESSOR	URGENT JOB	ARGUMENT
	1	2	3	4	5	6	7	8	9
1 OUT OF CONTROL – IN CONTROL	✓		✓		✓	✓		✓	✓

FIGURE 10

1 OUT OF CONTROL – IN CONTROL	✓	X	✓	X	✓	✓	O	✓	✓

FIGURE 11

mark with an 'O'.

Your first line will look something like figure 11:

STEP EIGHT

In this step you repeat the procedure you followed previously, except that you select a different three elements to consider.

This time the elements are:

4 5 6

Again ask yourself which two go together and which is the odd one out.

From your answer emerges your second construct. Try to find a different construct to your first answer. You may need to spend some time pondering over the way two of your elements go together. Listen to the answer which came immediately into your mind. You needn't accept it but do consider it; after all it came out of your head!

If you are stuck, here are some suggestions: be imaginative. If you could draw the elements, what shape, colour, form and size would they be. What pictures emerge? If you had to design a symbol for each, what comes into mind? Now which two seem to go together visually? What does the common denominator mean? Put it in words.

If you fail to find any pair which goes together, pick on what seems the odd one out (you just feel it is, but don't really know why). Ask yourself what qualities go with this odd-one-out element. For example if you have as an element: 'last year's holiday', you might write:

fun
no responsibility
relaxing
warmth
new
exciting
Select opposites to these:
fun ←————————→ boring
no responsibility ←————————→ worry
relaxing ←————————→ difficult

warmth ←——————————→ cold
new ←——————————→ dull
exciting ←——————————→ familiar

You can now select one of these constructs. Select the one which you feel is more important to you.

If you still find that you have got nowhere, simply move on to the next selection.

Again, as with your first construct, select your opposite. Do not bother with the dictionary opposite, unless it fits. Just put down what comes into your mind;

you can change it later if you wish.

For example you might write 'frustration' with an opposite as 'easy flow'. As long as you know what you mean that is all that matters.

Write your new constructs in the second row underneath your first selection, putting the negative construct on the left-hand side, as you did with your first selection. This will make it easy for you when you come to analyse your results:

Now tick all elements that link with your left-hand construct pole (that is frustration in the above example), cross

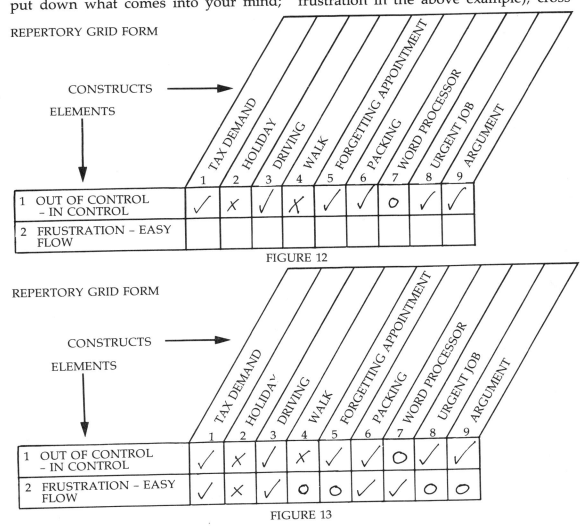

FIGURE 12

FIGURE 13

those which don't and put an 'O' for those which are in the middle or don't really apply.

You will now have something like figure 13.

Pause a moment and consider what your results mean. They show a small part of your world which is in some way connected with stress. In this example, let's say of Tom, he becomes stressed when he feels he cannot control the situation and also when things do not run smoothly.

Tom could spend some time looking at what control means to him. He could look at situations in which he feels he does not have control. It may be that there are ways in which he could exercise some control over at least part of them.

You can also see how Tom's belief limits his action: if he believes that he has no control, then he has no control – even if in reality there are things he could do. He won't even try. We limit ourselves by our thinking.

Another way Tom could look at this aspect of his stress problem is to consider more deeply what control means to him. To help there is a technique called laddering. This is how it works. Tom asks himself a series of questions like these:

'Why is it so important for me to be in control?'
Tom's answer:
'Because then I know what I'm doing'.
The next question is:

'Why is it important for me to know what I'm doing?'
The answer might be:
'Because then I am more sure of succeeding.'
Next question:
'Why is it important for me to succeed?'
Tom finds this difficult to answer. He feels that this is what he is supposed to do – succeed at all times.

When you ask yourself this set of questions and reach a level where you find it difficult to answer, you have reached what is called 'core' constructs. These are at the top of the hierarchy of your construct system.

Your construct system is the organization which contains all your constructs, their relationships with each other and the level of the relationship. Those at the top level are important. They are difficult to change. Later you will be able to see your part of your own construct system and how it is organized.

Let's return to Tom. He feels that he is the sort of person who is supposed to succeed. Tom next spends some time thinking about this, exploring all the implications connected with it (remember the loosening techniques discussed in the previous chapter).

Tom traces the idea that he must be a success back to other situations. He begins to see that it is a general principle in his life. As he looks further, he sees that although it is general, it seems to apply more when other people know whether he succeeds or not.

Tom realizes that he needs to be *seen* as a success. He starts to look at what failure means to him. He sees that he tends to label himself as a failure and to stop himself being reminded of what he feels himself to be underneath, he must present a façade to the world of being a success at all times.

Tom remembers how his father liked to talk about Tom's successes to relatives, even how his father would exaggerate. What seemed important was to *appear* successful.

Tom begins to consider what it would be like to reject this message behind these memories. He starts to examine how results are not usually black or white. He starts to take small risks which might end in failure. Tom eventually gets some movement into his life. He is not trapped by his past.

This was Tom's pathway. Yours may be quite different. Tracing back to the past may not be relevant. Your own exploration, although following similar lines, is likely to end in different results.

STEP NINE

Repeat the selection of elements (called triads) from your list, attempting to find different constructs.

This is the pattern for your selection:

construct number 3 from elements number 7, 8 and 9

4	1, 4 and 7
5	2, 5 and 8
6	3, 6 and 9
7	1, 5 and 9
8	3, 6 and 7
9	2, 4 and 8

Write each new construct (both poles) in the appropriate row of the grid form. Place the negative part of the construct on the left hand side.

Then add your ticks, crosses and 'Os'.

If you cannot find any new constructs, don't worry; leave out that triad selection and go on to the next one; or try the suggestions made earlier.

At the end of the exercise you should

REPERTORY GRID FORM

CONSTRUCTS ⟶

ELEMENTS

ELEMENTS / CONSTRUCTS	1 TAX DEMAND	2 HOLIDAY	3 DRIVING	4 WALK	5 FORGETTING APPOINTMENT	6 PACKING	7 WORD PROCESSOR	8 URGENT JOB	9 ARGUMENT
1 OUT OF CONTROL – IN CONTROL	✓	X	✓	X	✓	✓	O	✓	✓
2 FRUSTRATION – EASY FLOW	✓	X	✓	O	O	✓	✓	O	O
3 UNABLE TO EXPRESS ANGER – OPEN ANGER	X	X	O	X	✓	O	X	✓	✓
4 IMPERSONAL – PERSONAL	✓	X	X	X	X	O	O	X	✓
5 SEEN AS INEFFICIENT – NOT SO	X	O	✓	O	✓	O	O	✓	O
6 SERIOUS CONSQUENCES – NOT SO SERIOUS	✓	X	✓	X	✓	X	X	✓	O
7 PROCRASTINATE – GET ON WITH IT	✓	X	✓	O	O	✓	✓	O	O
8 POOR END RESULTS – GOOD RESULTS	✓	X	✓	X	✓	✓	O	✓	✓
9 TIME CONTROLLED BY OTHERS – OWN USE OF TIME	✓	X	✓	X	✓	✓	O	✓	✓

FIGURE 14

have a list of nine constructs, something like the example in figure 14.

STEP TEN

Now comes an important part. This is where you look for constructs which are linked together to form patterns. You do this by looking at lines which are the same or similar; that is where the rows are the same or quite similar (allow up to two differences).

You can do this visually by just guessing which link together and then checking if you are correct. Another way is to copy out the first line and then run it downwards so that you can compare line 1 with all the other lines.

You then copy out line 2 and compare it with line 3, 4 and all subsequent lines.

Repeat the process by copying out line 3 and comparing it with lines 4, 5 and 6 etc. This is a bit time consuming. Another method is to colour all your crosses red, your ticks green and leave the 'Os' white. This should enable you to easily see the connections (unless you are colour blind).

Most people find a visual check sufficient.

Later chapters show you more sophisticated ways of analysing grids. Your own visual analysis will, however, give you sufficient information about the pattern of stressors in your life. The really important thing is the process itself. As you go through the exercises eliciting constructs and examining their meaning, you gain insights which help you deal with stress in your life.

If you look at the last example, you can see that lines 1, 8 and 9 are similar. Lines 2 and 7 link together. Other lines do not really fit anywhere else.

In our example 'out of control', 'poor end results' and 'time controlled by others' link together.

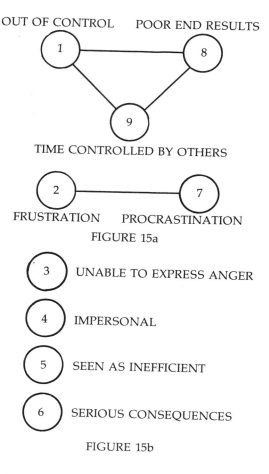

FIGURE 15a

FIGURE 15b

Another cluster is 'frustration' and 'procrastination'.

To help you see the relationships more easily, you can draw the links:

3, 4, 5 and 6 are all separate.

You can now examine the constructs which are linked together. They may be linked coincidentally but it is more likely they have a common factor which combines them.

See if you can provide a name for each combination of clusters. One of the existing constructs within the cluster may be particularly important and this can be used to provide the name for the whole cluster; or you may think of a different name which would be more suitable to cover all the constructs within one combination.

Providing a name is an important exercise. It tells you the underlying concept which links constructs. If you then examine these meta-constructs, you begin to tackle stress at a deeper, wider and more powerful level.

In the example 1, 8 and 9 seem to be connected with getting things done, or with hindrances to getting things done.

The second cluster appears to be around the area of movement. In fact if you look at all five constructs, there seems to be an overall common link. The differences between 1, 2, 7, 8 and 9 are not that great.

We could redraw them with a lighter line connecting the first three to the two others:

Here we have an important area of stress all connected with getting things done and being hindered in some way.

We could give a common name to this even larger cluster: frustration.

With its opposite we have:

frustration ◄──────► getting things done

This now opens up a major area to explore. The exploration starts with seeing how many stress-events are connected with the new construct. In this example it seems that most of the stress is caused by not getting things done.

The next step is to ladder the construct to see its hidden and deeper meaning.

The questioning technique has already been outlined. You ask yourself why it is so important to get things done without hindrance.

The answer might be:

'Then I feel free'.

This area of needing to be free and of feeling trapped is then explored. Ideas about not living my own life might emerge. You then look at what living your own life means. List what you really want out of your life. Look at all the incidents which seem to be connected with this construct to see how general it is in your life. It may be connected with most things, or only with events at work or when you are with your family.

Trace back to earlier incidents which seem connected. Would you give the construct a somewhat different name when applied to these earlier events. If so, what is the difference between the two? Go back to even earlier times and modify its names if appropriate. You may, for instance, find that it is connected with being allowed free time after you have achieved your school (or other childhood) tasks; or that when things weren't working out for you, that your mother always stepped in and helped you. You may still be living within these guidelines.

You may be working on the assumption that everything *should* flow freely. When you consider this, you begin to realize that life cannot be like this. It is not organized so that you get what you want when you want it.

You then begin to see frustration differently, consider what aspects of your job could be changed and what new skills would help. Many different factors emerge. You realize that you tend to take on more work than you can handle so

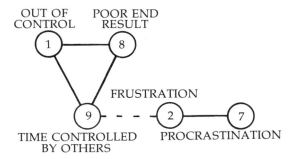

OUT OF CONTROL · POOR END RESULT

1 · 8

FRUSTRATION

9 · 2 · 7

TIME CONTROLLED BY OTHERS · PROCRASTINATION

FIGURE 16

that you actually create frustration for yourself. It might help for you to learn to become more assertive and say 'no' when asked to do something when you are already busy.

Eventually you see your work hindrances as problems to be solved. You free energy, enabling you to tackle problems productively. They cease to be stressors in your life.

What this examination does is to open up new ways of seeing things. This leads you to explore new angles which help provide creative solutions to your problems.

You may find that your problems are centred around 'having to be responsible', or your concept of 'the good mother', or about conflict between needing to be free and accepting the constraints of family life. You may find that you have to face important choices about whether to stay in a relationship or get out.

Your stress may be connected with being stuck and you have remained stuck because you feared facing the consequences of making choices. You may find that you are trapped because you accept a lot of 'shoulds' in your life. 'I should be slimmer'. 'I should be able to do those things'. 'I should not be so angry with my son'. 'I should be more loving'.

Examine what you are being forced into. If you are overweight and feel unhealthy, then it is a good idea to diet but not to do so to fit in with images created by fashion magazines or because someone else tells you what sort of weight you must be.

Seek out what you really want out of life. As a child did you have an idea of how your life was to turn out? What was your favourite fairy story – what was its central message and what does this say about your present day life? Do you have a recurrent dream? If so what again is the message or the main character? Examine what relevance these have to your life at present.

Move to the end of your life and imagine it has been a play. What sort did it turn out to be? Comedy? Tragedy? Farce? One long bore?

It is important to realize that your constructs are likely to be different from the examples provided. Your combinations will also differ. You may find that everything is related to everything else or that nothing fits together.

If all your constructs are related, problems with one are likely to affect all others. Look at your negative constructs. This is the price you are paying for not getting what you need out of life.

If your constructs are not linked, then you have to work through each separately.

If most of your stressors are connected with work, you can turn to the section on work-related stress and look even deeper in that particular area.

There is another powerful exercise which helps you to examine how your life fits together and that is script analysis taken from Transactional Analysis.

These are the questions you ask yourself:

1 Who was the person most significant to you when you were a child?

2 Write three things you liked about that person.

3 Write three things you did not like.

4 Which was easier, 2 or 3, to answer? How did you feel about listing positive qualities? And negative ones?

5 How did that person treat you when you were ill?

6 How did that person treat you when you were naughty?

7 If you had to state a message that that person gave you about how to live your life, what would it be? The message may have been clearly stated or only in-

ferred by you. It may have been straightforward or confusing.

8 How does that message affect your present day life?

9 If your life was a TV play, what sort would it be – a comedy, tragedy, boring, one long laugh, a farce or what?

10 At the end of your life, what message might appear on your tombstone which sums up who you were?

11 Hidden at the back of the tombstone so that no one can see, is another message about you, what does it say?

See where these questions lead. You may surprise yourself.

It helps to talk through what emerges with someone you know who is understanding. It helps also to keep a record of your thoughts and ideas as they emerge. Working through these exercises usually reveals many factors which need to be followed up. So make a note of them at the time they emerge so that you can return to them later.

Remember also that professional help is available. If you feel you would benefit from seeing a counsellor or therapist, you can contact some of the addresses mentioned at the end of the book.

What you have been doing is to extract from concrete situations or events in your world meaning behind those which trigger a stress response. You looked at how these meanings are linked together and then at the implications of what they mean in your life at present, in the past and in the future.

You begin to re-examine these meanings. Although this seems easy in print, it can be threatening in real life. If your stress is connected with accepting responsibilities which are almost impossible to fulfil, you cannot give them up that easily. Growth and change is painful but once you start the process, you begin to feel that your life is moving once again

and realize the worthwhileness of what you are doing. You also need to understand that, through your own efforts, by taking responsibility for your life, you have refashioned a more satisfactory way of living.

Taking responsibility for yourself, your condition and circumstances, is an important factor. It may be tough but it is your way to a more constructive life.

Much of the discussion has been about loosening, that is opening up, letting ideas flow and being creative. You need to tighten things up, otherwise you'll have masses of insight and ideas but little change in the external world. You need to see how your constructs have (or could be) changed and test out new behaviour.

Do not move from one extreme to another, try out a slightly different type of behaviour which is not too threatening. For instance, if you find that you go out very little, do not join every club and society there is in your neighbourhood, but start to talk to people you meet or select one evening class or club to attend.

Once you've tried alternative behaviour, review how you feel about it. You may not like what you've done, or you may decide to make it permanently part of the way you live. What you will learn is that you can change and that you do have power over your life.

This is not a one-off process with a 'here is the solution to all your problems'. It is part of a cycle or (better still) a spiral. Your repertory grid gives a direction for exploration. Loosening exercises create new possibilities. Tightening enables you to test things out. What would it be like if it was... You find out. You might then return to loosening and repeat the process. You can retake your repertory grid and see what changes have taken place. Select another area to work through and by so doing you enrich your life even more.

LIST OUT THE MAJOR STRESS AREAS:

1 _____

2 _____

3 _____

4 _____

5 _____

FIGURE 17

The important point is to consider the exercise as a *process*. It is dynamic, not static.

If (and this is likely) you find that there are many stressors in your life, select one area to work on first. Do not attempt to tackle everything. The rest will have to wait.

Add the goals that you would like to achieve in each area. Be specific and realistic. Concentrate on solutions not problems.

Look at what you have written from many angles. Examine the positive aspects of so-called negative qualities. If your life is constricted and you cut yourself off from people because you find that relating to others is a major stress area in your life, you might conclude that this is a way of caring for yourself. Within the way you see things, it is effective and positive.

Also, you may not want to move into a world of parties, social activities and frequent contact with others – only to be able to relate to others on limited occasions. You may be a private person who prefers her or his own company. This is fine. You do not have to force yourself into a social role you dislike. The German word for 'loneliness' is 'einsamheit' but it does not have the same negative connotation as the English meaning has. Some people only feel that they should be more gregarious because this is how they think society feels people should be.

Change is not swinging from one end of a construct to the opposite pole but is much more subtle. In fact you may reject a construct totally as it no longer applies.

Evaluate what you have written. Ask yourself how realistic are your objectives. Ask yourself who is pushing you into them. If you say this is how it should be, question the statement: who says so?

Consider the barriers that stop you getting what you want. How real are they? Think of different ways of overcoming them. If you feel that you have no energy to tackle them, ask yourself what this is saying to you. It may be that you don't want the goals you have set yourself.

The objectives you have written down probably have a negative side. Things are not usually black or white but many shades in between or even black *and* white. Face the negative parts. Many of us do not just love someone, we may hate them at times as well. We may like some aspects of their character and yet dislike other parts. If we try only to love, we may find the suppressed parts becoming more powerful and blotting out love.

Spend some time listening to yourself. Don't be afraid of hearing what you're saying.

A client of mine was stuck in her life. She fought hard to control what was happening to her but it did not seem to work. She had to fight harder and harder. What her inner voice was saying was: 'let go and fall in love.' You have an inner wisdom which is telling you something important.

Ask yourself what your stress is saying to you. Imagine it is a person. What would it say? Isn't it shouting something important? Let it speak for once. Perhaps your stress is located in a particular part of your body. What does this say to you – you haven't got a leg to stand on, it is a pain in the neck, the whole thing makes me sick, I am stiff with unexpressed anger or ache with unsaid statements.

When you're clear about your goals and have selected one or two to concentrate on, work out alternative ways of achieving them. Break down your activities into small manageable steps. Include different ways of reaching these as well.

When you have set yourself a direction and started your journey, it may well be that you will change your mind. And that is how it should be. Without starting, you would have got nowhere and you would not have chosen the path that you eventually took.

If stress is connected with a major negative event in your life, you need to work somewhat differently.

Often such events are connected with loss. You need to accept your loss. Own it, fully and completely. This means all the feelings connected with it. They may not only be sadness. They could contain anger, hatred, fear, pity, love – all mixed up together.

Trust yourself by accepting whatever surfaces by letting it emerge. You feel like crying or raging. Do it. Let it be. If you find you distance yourself from the event, start to recall various aspects of it. Look at photographs of your dead husband or the old home. Go over in your mind the times you had together, bad ones and good ones. Let feelings flow from these memories.

Do not fight sadness. There is a time to be depressed. Take into yourself what is meaningful – your loneliness, sorrow or regret. Accept it. This may seem cruel. In a way it is. But these emotions are the realities of the situation. They haven't been worked through. They are in the way of you moving on in your life.

You require time. You need also to face up to working on how you are going to live the rest of your life. You have to say goodbye to the past. You have to face creating your future. There is also a reality to your life. If you are holding on to the past, it may be because the future is too threatening. You have to face it all alone. You have to look after the house, deal with all financial matters, face problems – alone. So to be safe, you remain in the past.

You can – gently at first – begin to examine what your new situation really means. Before you were a couple. Now you are independent. As in some of the previous examples, start to explore what this means, what your fears are, what aspects you feel most vulnerable about.

If stressful situations cause you to panic, tremble, sweat, feel dizzy and think you are not in control, accept these feelings. They will pass. Often it is the fear of fear that is the problem. If you accept your fear, it will not build up. It becomes manageable.

Start to tackle smaller things to begin

with. Also allow yourself to develop aspects of your personality which have hitherto been suppressed. You are allowed desires and wishes. You can permit yourself new possibilites.

Let's see where we have reached:

1 You have explored situations which stress you and the meaning you give to these. Often this is sufficient to get you moving once again in your life. The actual process of working through reconstruing and examining alternatives releases feeling and associated memories. These trigger off further memories and emotions.

2 You have started to build competencies which help you deal with your new perceptions.

3 You have tried out new behaviours.

There is another important step to take. That is to learn to relax. Connected with all types of stress is arousal. Relaxation reduces this. It also counteracts some of the adverse physiological effects of stress. The pressures will ease and this will enable you to view things differently. The next chapter shows you how but, before this, we need to look at a more complex cause of stress. This is connected not with external triggers so much but with conflicts *within* a person.

STRESS AND THE CONFLICT WITHIN . . .

At the beginning of this chapter we discussed how stress results from events which are perceived as containing some form of threat. Threat arises because we feel that we do not have the inner or external resources to deal with it adequately. We feel obliged to do what needs to be done. We may, of course, have the capacity to tackle things effectively but we believe that it will be too much for us. We act within this belief – that we are at-tempting to cope with something which is too much for us.

For some, the matter is even more complicated. Part of our personality may see fulfilment in particular events and situations. We seek them because of the way they satisfy us. But somewhere within us, other parts rebel. What we are doing is exactly what 'they' do not want. It may work the other way around. We avoid taking on challenging work, feeling that we are not up to it, but some aspect of our personality craves excitement. We deny ourselves what we could be.

The conflict is not a straightforward one of us versus a situation but an inner battle. We want what we avoid.

The tough, thrusting, successful entrepreneur, in whose psyche is hidden a romantic. The housewife who has the strengths of a successful businesswoman hidden by a veneer of weaknesses that she presents to the world and to herself most of the time. What we fear are our strengths not just our weaknesses.

These parts of ourselves can be suppressed and sometimes almost completely hidden. We say: 'I was not myself...' We were, of course, ourselves – who else could we be? We are taken by surprise as a hidden part of our mental life is occasionally liberated.

Placed in a dark corner of our minds, these aspects of our personalities have power. They nag away at us. They pull us away from what we want to do. They do so because we refuse them expression.

They are not just negative and weak. They may hold growth pointers for our lives. They hold directions for us to travel and experiences for us to explore. To examine them, and the meanings they have in relation to the they way we live, is not only to remove stress but is to stop denying ourselves something of what we could be. Through them we find a deeper identity.

This idea of different parts of a personality is not new. Over four hundred years ago, Montaigne wrote:

'We are all made up of fragments and strangely assembled so that, every moment, every piece plays its own game. There is as much difference between us and ourselves as between us and others.'

Plato suggests an analogy of a person as a city state and Henry Murray says: 'A person is a full congress of orators'. Alexander David Niel goes further stating that '...fellow members may come to blows'. Christopher Isherwood has written of human life as: '...a pattern of selves'.

Somerset Maugham sensed domination of one part of ourselves over another when he wrote: 'We are made up of several persons and at any moment one person has the upper hand'. Gurdjieff talks of: 'Man (being) divided into multiplicities of small "I's"...this explains why one "I" decides but action may be the business of another "I", which is not in favour of the decision'.

In a poem Pablo Neruda writes of dozing in the midst of people of distinction and of summoning up his courageous self when:

... a coward completely unknown to me swaddles my poor skeleton in a thousand tiny reservations.

These different parts of our personality have often been called 'sub-personalities'. The title is a good one. It indicates that they have a certain completeness so that they could be recognized as persons if we met and interacted with them but also that they miss something. They are only 'sub', that is part of something larger. We are more than a collection of sub-personalities. It also suggests that living through one or a few sub-personalities is to ignore our full potential as a human being.

In Personal Construct Psychology terms, sub-personalities can be thought of as a special type of sub-system, within our overall construct system, which is sufficiently homogeneous to be recognized by us and others as a complete (but limited) personality. Certain traits and constructs are clustered to produce a semblance of unity.

Many other psychological systems have similar ideas. In psychoanalysis, Grotstein describes as a defence mechanism part of the total personality being split off and becoming relatively autonomous, following its own way of life. It is the *lack* of integration that enables us to exist. Parts of ourselves are denied expression because, if they were externalized, we feel at some level of awareness that the conflict would be too great for us.

Sullivan thought of the self as being made up of a mirror within us reflecting how others view us and that some of these images may be 'false personifications'.

Berger sees human behaviour as drama: we are different actors in different situations and there are parts we play both within ourselves and with others. He also says that some identities are temporary and trivial and not too difficult to change but some are very difficult to alter.

Jung's archetypes may be thought of as sub-personalities which are common to most people. The wise old man, perhaps trapping us with his apparent wisdom; the anima and animus – the male side of females and vice versa, existing in us but denied expression. Men are not supposed to be kind, loving, nurturing and caring, nor women, tough and powerful. The shadow, that dark part of ourselves – powerful because we deny its existence.

In analytical psychology, these aspects are worked through (the process is called individuation) until the self can incorporate them. They are transformed and so is the total personality. You look at the opposites in yourself and work so that these are integrated into your total personality.

Transactional Analysis (which was mentioned earlier in this chapter) suggests that we all have three ego states called Parent, Adult and Child. Some of us spend most of our time, for example, in our Critical Parent. We deny our Child and the fun and spontaneity we could have in our life.

Gestalt has its top and under dogs; when we are tough we are reminded about how weak we are. Psychosynthesis relies heavily on the concept of sub-personalities. The whole is made up of many parts, in each of us there is a diversity of semi-autonomous sub-personalities, all striving to express themselves.

There are also cases of multiple personalities, where one part of a person may not realize the existence of other parts.

In a later chapter on stress and work, the roles we play and how they can lead to stress is discussed. Sub-personalities are related to, but different from roles.

The word 'role' usually means a bundle of related expectations about behaviour and attitudes about particular social positions and situations. This might be about the role of a doctor, a father, diners in a restaurant, passengers in an aircraft and so on. There are role sets: doctor-patient, waiter-diner, husband-wife and so on. A patient does not enter a dentist's surgery and pull out the teeth of the dentist!

Problems arise through many aspects of role:

1 Role conflict – for example the public stereotyped image of the nurse conflicting with the expectations of the hospital and the nurse's own awareness that she cannot humanly meet all demands and that her own interests conflict anyway. The same applies to police, medical personnel, teachers and others.

2 Role ambiguity – being uncertain of what is required is a major cause of stress according to recent studies. We feel comfortable if we know what we are supposed to do.

Robert Ornstein in his book *Multimind*, says that we are a coalition, not a single person and that we have a multiplicity of small and separate minds.

Sub-personalities are construct sub-systems which are complete enough to act as real persons. Sub-personalities seek certain roles, perhaps delight in them and devote their energies into performing to meet all expectations. This can be, however, to the detriment of what other sub-personalities wish.

One client of mine was totally caught up in the 'good-mother' role because this is all that one of her sub-personalities wanted. Another sub-personality named 'artist', wanted freedom, to do its own thing and to reject the mother role. The 'mother' sub-personality pushed the client into meeting all the obligations of the mother role.

She denied the 'artistic' side of herself, resulting in her beginning to hate her mother-role. She saw things as either/or. She must be a good mother or throw it all up. To do so (in fact even to think about doing so) meant guilt – she was not the sort of person she thought she should be. By initially looking at what the 'artist' was saying to her and then allowing it some space in her life, she was able to reduce stress in her life.

The theoretical aspects of the concept of sub-personalities need not concern us. They may or may not be actual aspects of personality. The important point is that they are *useful*. By using the idea, you can get hold of and examine parts of your personality which are held back. You consider things *as if* they were so. You bring conflict into the open. You listen to what repressed parts of you are saying to you. You can then work through and release energies that you have invested in coping with stress. You find new aspects of yourself which enrich your life.

Here's how you can start to examine sub-personalities in your life:

1 Is there a recurrent theme, character or pattern to some of your dreams?

2 What do you daydream of, is there any pattern to these?

3 Do you feel part of you wishes to pull you in a different direction in your life?

4 Is part of you in the way of where you want to go?

5 Have you ever said: 'I wasn't myself when I did that', or have you acted out of character?

6 Have you ever caught fleeting glimpses of yourself – perhaps as you've seen your reflection in a shop window and felt as if what you've seen is a stranger?

7 Do you feel that you are different people?

The next step is to breathe some life into these shadowy figures. Give them a name. I know this may seem silly but try it. If you have a dream with a recurrent theme, what name would you give to that theme if it were a person?

For instance if your theme was one of always being hindered in what you're attempting to achieve, what name would you give to that hindrance. It might be an actual personal name like 'John', or a name that represents it, such as 'The Hindrance'.

If you give it a personal name, ask yourself why you gave it that name. Explore what ideas come into your mind. Write them down. Sum up what they are saying to you.

Now go further and let the sub-personality say what it wants to say about itself. Just talk as if the sub-personality was a real person. Let the words come out of your mouth.

You might find something like:

'Yes, I get in your way. I stop you doing things because I don't want to do them. All you do is to push and push and push. I am sick of it. I want some peace. Some time for rest and to think about things. I feel that I am being pushed so far in a direction that all I want out of life will be missed.'

This message is saying something important. Go further and say that you are clear about the protest but exactly what does the sub-personality want, what would it do if it had the time and peace it desires?

You might get:

'I want peace so that I can think things out and explore new directions. I want to change the pace of life and spend time clarifying some issues which are important. I would like to write and to share my ideas with others....'

Try fantasy. Let your mind wander as your subpersonality lives its life. Where does your imagination lead you?

Try to categorize your sub-personalities: are they from the past or do they point to the future; are they about everyday things in the 'here and now' or more in the imagination; are they clear or dark and shadowy? Do you feel that they are negative or positive? Have they been around for many years or just recently entered your life? If they came in recently, what was it that triggered their entry?

Now, of course, your sub-personalities may be quite different from these examples and their messages point elsewhere. You have to trust yourself – and *listen* to what is being said.

You may find that a number of sub-personalities emerge. Let them have a meeting. Allow each of them to state its case. Do not push them back because you are disgusted, or fear what may arise.

Mair sees the self as a community with sub-personalities not existing in isolation but with a community of selves. He describes them as a metaphor, useful as long as we do not let it trap or constrict us. It is a means to an end. It is a way of experiencing potentialities and a way of grasping aspects of the unknown and exploring them.

If a lot of negative qualities emerge, seek some positive aspects of them. For example, you may find that one sub-personality is self-indulgent and lazy.

What are the good qualities of such traits? They might include: rewarding you, making you feel good, enabling you to rest or to have a good time.

Go a stage further and write out the sort of life one of your sub-personalities would have if it were allowed full expression. Go beyond the obvious. Where would it live, with whom, what sort of job, how would it dress, where would it go on vacation, what about its hobbies, would it be religious? What do you dislike about any of these things – and like about some of them?

As you do the exercise, what feelings emerge in you?

Another approach is through a repertory grid.

Use each sub-personality as an element. Say you have five or six, select numbers 1, 2 and 3 and ask which two are more alike and in what way.

This is one pole of your first construct. Now decide what its opposite is. This is important because it may contain the quality you fear most.

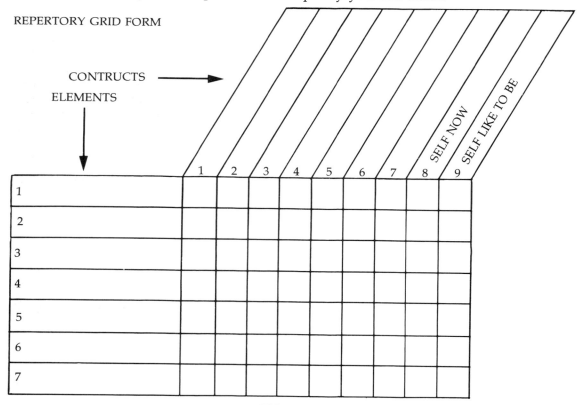

REPERTORY GRID FORM

FIGURE 18

Repeat the exercise with numbers:

```
4 5 6
1 2 4
1 2 5
1 2 6
2 4 6
3 4 5
```

You should have seven constructs. Do not worry if you have less (or more). Place them in the grid (figure 18). You will see that two other elements have been added:

self-now
self-like-to-be.

Where the first pole of a construct links with an element place a tick in the box under it. If it does not link, place a cross there. If it is in the middle put an 'O' in the box as you did in previous exercises.

Follow the procedures outlined earlier and see which constructs are linked. Examine carefully which ones link with 'self-now' and 'self-like-to-be'. Which are closer to yourself now and which represent qualities you'd like to have in the future. What does this say about your life?

You can also look at how your various sub-personalities are related by seeing how the elements are linked together.

From your grid, list the qualities of each sub-personality as if you were writing a brief sketch about them. Use the constructs as descriptions:

'Jeremy is the weak side of me. He never seems to be able to do anything well. He doesn't want to try. He seems to be pulling me all the time to give up. He is dull, shy, introverted and frightened.'

Go further and imagine their preferences in clothes, cars, food, books, favourite hates and so on.

Compare descriptions of sub-personalities with each other. Some may be opposites. Others link in no way – positively or negatively.

Now think how, within limits, you could let a sub-personality 'be' you for a week or so. As this is threatening, place a protective boundary on full expression. And also have a time limit.

After your 'role enactment', review how you felt. After you've tried out your new personality, you can retain or discard parts. You've shown yourself that you can change.

The process is:

symbol →sub-personality →role enactment →real life living.

The symbol may be strong or quite weak. You flesh it out into more of a person. This enables you to look at it, grasp it and explore it in more detail. Role enactment is letting it or part of it be you for a week or so.

One client asked for help because she lost her voice. No physical reason had been found. What emerged was that the lost voice covered up the fact that she couldn't eat. This she hid from almost everyone with considerable skill. The client was a thirty-seven year old successful businesswoman who had made the grade despite tremendous opposition (mostly from males in her firm). Outwardly she was successful, aggressive, competitive, decisive and results orientated.

From a repertory grid a number of constructs emerged which suggested a potential sub-personality. She called one her 'soft-self'. It was vulnerable, disorganized and frightened. With some difficulty, she elaborated by letting the sub-personality say what it wanted. It told her how it wanted to live and what needs it felt must be met.

It was all about the client rejecting herself as a woman by denying feelings because she felt that to express them would mean she would be taken advantage of. Her message was a strong plea which she had always suppressed by becoming even more dynamic and competitive. So the shouting had to be louder and the conflict and stress more intense.

It was not a question of giving up her present day life but of listening to herself and then being willing to allow some external expression of what was being said. What she really wanted was to enter into a relationship. She let herself do so and eventually found a way of still being a fairly forceful businesswoman *and* some one who could be soft and gentle.

When the power of hidden needs is released, the results need not be a compromise but a creative synthesis. It is, also, amazing how in most of us we have the answers to our problems.

Looking at sub-personalities in your life can reduce stress but there is much more to it than that. There is an excitement about living once again and of experiencing something of what you could be.

TOPIC REFERENCES

Community of selves:
Mair, J. M. M., 'The community of selves', in *New perspectives* and *Metaphors for Living* at Nebraska Symposium on Motivation (1976), 1977.

Hassles and stress:
Kanner, A.D. et al, *Daily Hassles*, Journal of Behavioural Medicine, 4, 1981.

Laddering:
Hinkle, D., *The change of personal constructs from the viewpoint of a theory of construct implications*. Unpublished PhD thesis, Ohio State University, 1965.

Sub Personalities:
Psychosynthesis:
Assogioli, R., *Psychosynthesis*, Turnstone Books, 1975.

Transactional Analysis:
Berne, E., *Transactional analysis in psychotherapy*. Grove Press, 1976.

Psychoanalysis:
Grotstein, J., *Splitting and projective identification*. Quoted in *Changes*, PPA, 1984.
Gurdjieff, J. Quoted by John Rowen in *Ordinary ecstasy*, Routledge & Kegan Paul, 1976.
Maugham, S. Quoted by T. A. Harris in *I'm OK, you're OK*, Pan Books, 1969.
Neruda, P. 1970. 'We are many' in *Selected poems*, Penguin 1972.
Perl, F., *Gestalt therapy verbatim*, Penguin, 1978.
Ornstein, R., *Multiminds*. Macmillan, 1986.

CHAPTER 4

Learning to relax

When you looked at the stressors in your life, found how they linked together and the meaning they had for you in your life, you made a major advance in tackling stress.

By examining your personal patterns of stress-inducing events, you are able to start tackling them at their source. Your analysis provides you with insights which help direct your efforts and enable you to start to develop alternative ways of seeing things – ways which need not trap you into helplessness. From this you explore new ways of dealing with problems. You see them in a different light.

Stress we described as being a combination of:

1 Event, situation or circumstance, present, past or anticipated; real or imagined.

2 Your perception or cognition of that event which includes some form of threat with which you feel you do not have adequate resources to cope easily or at all.

3 The way you physiologically respond to your perception of that event or situation.

4 Your behaviour which is your attempt to cope, even if it is to run away or avoid the situation.

Your behaviour, in turn, becomes an event which feeds back into the system and further increases your stress. You see that you are unable to deal with the situation effectively and this in itself is stress-inducing.

In daily living, the middle two parts (2 and 3) are combined. You perceive some form of overt or covert threat in a situation and this sets in motion a series of parallel physiological processes.

Common to all stress is physiological arousal. You may be more alert – or over-alert; ready to fight or flee – but often the best response to a difficult situation is to take time, consider things carefully and develop options about how to deal with things. Instead of that, you find it difficult to think straight. You act in haste. You attack when it is better to remain calm. Or you run away when you need to face things. This may include actually removing yourself from the stress-inducing event or pretending it is not there. Such physical responses helped our ancestors survive an attack from a wild animal. We, however, face very different problems.

Sometimes the system is the other way around. We start at the physiological end. A chemical imbalance causes us to feel irritable, anxious or aroused in some way and we seek (or there already exists) a suitable event in the environment which provides us with a rationale which fits our pre-existing mood.

In a series of experiments in the 1960s an American psychologist, Stanley Schachter, was able to fashion the mood of subjects already aroused with a drug by manipulating the environment. He was able to make some subjects euphoric and others angry. Being aroused, subjects sought cues in their immediate surroundings to provide reasons why they felt as they did. If these cues suggested that they should be angry, they became angry; if cues made euphoria a more suitable mood, they stated that they felt really good about things. Most of us have had the experience of someone close to us just looking for a fight. We look outside us for something which will enable us to channel our physiological arousal into an appropriate emotion.

An allergy to food or other substances can sometimes be the cause. People may be allergic to certain fruits, milk or other foods. The body, in the process of trying to adapt, releases adrenaline and this starts a stress-like process.

If you feel generally stressed and irritable and when you examine the meanings behind the stressors in your life you still feel that the way you see things is insufficient to warrant your reactions, you might like to consider the food you eat. If you eat a bland diet of pears and lamb for a week, your body will lose its capacity to adapt to the guilty food and when you do eat whatever it is that is at the root of the problem, you will get a powerful reaction. By adding different foods to your diet, you will discover which cause problems. You need to avoid those foods in the future.

Other substances can also trigger similar difficulties – plastics, car fumes, perfumes, material and detergents etc.

It is likely, however, that stress results from a number of factors. The main input is likely be an external event which is perceived in a way as threatening and this triggers off the stress response. If you are already allergic to certain foods or chemicals, your base level for being able to tackle things effectively is already low.

You start vulnerable. What might have been a minor problem a few years ago now seems something impossible to con-

trol. You are affected by an initial stressor. When you are presented with additional difficulties, you feel less able to tackle them. Like a rolling snowball, your stress increases as you proceed throughout the day.

The mood fashioned by initial stressors lingers and is projected onto even more situations. A bad day at the office and you arrive home ready to snap at the slightest thing. You feel bad about your outburst and this adds to the existing work-induced stress. You don't recuperate from the strains of your job during the evening. You are doubly stressed. Problems press their unfinished business as you try to sleep. The next day, unrested, further battles have to be faced. Gradually your immune system becomes weakened. Illness is more frequent. Your capacity to tackle difficult life events is even further impeded.

Stress needs to be tackled holistically. Two major ways which assist are to pinpoint specific stressors and to reduce arousal.

Relaxation helps in two ways. By becoming more calm and relaxed each day the general stress level is reduced. Long-term negative effects are also reduced. You begin to feel better, you find you have more energy and this, in itself, changes the way you see things.

Being able to relax each day helps you deal with problems more competently.

This chapter aims to help you do these two things.

Relaxation is a skill. Like other skills it needs to be practised. It takes time but it is worth it. By relaxing each day you begin to reverse many of the adverse long effects of stress. Your immune system improves so that you are able to resist germs and viruses more powerfully.

You need to set up your own personal relaxation training programme. The first stage is a learning one. The second is to make relaxation a habit. The third stage is to learn how to relax in difficult situations.

A cassette is available from bookshops or the publishers of this book (the address is on the cover) which you can use to help you relax. This is worth getting as it will make it easier for you. Of course, you must never use any relaxation cassette or carry out the exercises when you are driving a car. If you are prone to suffer from epileptic fits you need to check with your doctor whether it is all right for you to pratise relaxation as sometimes fits occur when you reach a relaxed state as you do just before you fall asleep.

The following instructions may look complicated but if you take them a few at a time, you will find that you can become skilled relatively quickly.

1 Find a comfortable place to sit. Make sure your back is upright and comfortable. You will need a place where you will not be disturbed. You can lie down but if you feel tired you are likely to fall asleep. This is fine if you want to sleep. Certainly, a relaxed half-hour sleep is refreshing but by sitting up you are likely to remain in a state similar to the comfortable, drowsy state you feel just before you fall asleep. Just let whatever happens happen. You don't have to try. Let things happen.

2 Just relax yourself as far as you can. Note any parts of your body which are tense and relax these. Take your time.

3 Take a deep breath and slowly breathe out to the count of five – one, two, three, four, five. Allow yourself to relax as you do so. As you count and breathe out, imagine that you are relaxing. Do it slowly. You will need to practise this a few times until you feel yourself relaxing as you breathe out.

4 Repeat this a few times until you feel quite calm and relaxed.

5 Count backwards: five, four, three, two, one and when you reach 'one' look upwards with your eyes open as if you are looking through the back of your head or the top of your eyebrows. Don't strain your head by bending it upwards – just let your eyes look upwards. Pause.

6 Count: one, two, three, four, five and close your eyes as you reach 'five'. Let yourself relax. Pause and slowly let the whole of your body relax. Remain like this for a few moments.

7 Count: five, four, three, two, one and open your eyes and again look upwards and through the back of your head. Don't let your head strain backwards, just your eyes looking upwards. Pause. Your eyes are likely to ache a little at this stage.

8 Count up again: one, two, three, four, five. Close your eyes and as you do so say to yourself that you are becoming twice as relaxed as you were previously. Just say it quietly to yourself. Let the relaxation spread through the whole of your body. Imagine it happening. Gently tell your face that it is twice as relaxed as it was previously, then your neck, shoulders, arms, hands, body, legs and feet. Take your time. Remain like this for a few moments.

9 Count: five, four, three, two, one and look upwards and backwards again as you did previously. Pause. Your eyes will feel heavy and you will find it difficult to keep them open. But do keep them open even if they ache a little. Stay like this for a few seconds.

10 Count: one, two, three, four, five and close your eyes and say to yourself that you are becoming ten times as relaxed as you were previously. Repeat quietly and slowly a few times – that you are becoming ten times as relaxed as you were previously. Just imagine each main part of your body relaxing deeply. Take

your time. You don't have to try. Just let things happen.

11 Feel yourself relaxed and mentally go through each part of your body from your head down again saying how relaxed it is. Remain like this for a few moments. You will find that thoughts come into your mind. This is fine. Do not stop them, just let them come and go without any effort on your part.

12 Count backwards from 300 (ie 299, 298, 297 and so on) and as you do so imagine that your mind is becoming as relaxed as your body. Just continue to count until you feel mentally relaxed and then let the numbers go.....

13 Now imagine that you are going to relax to three levels which are even deeper than the state that you are in so far:

Level one. Allow yourself to go down to level one (if it helps imagine yourself floating gently and effortlessly down) and when you feel you've reached level one –

allow yourself to go down to level two, which is deeper still than level one. Take your time. Again imagine that you are floating down into level two. You might visualize a notice which says: 'Level Two'. Allow yourself to experience how relaxed you feel. When you sense you've reached level two:

Let yourself go down to the deepest level of all – level three. Take your time. This time imagine that you are virtually weightless, just lightly floating down from a very relaxed state to an even deeper one. When you have reached this state, allow yourself to remain there and experience what it is like to feel so peaceful and relaxed.

14 Finally imagine yourself in a very pleasant place, a garden or a beach or a quiet peaceful scene from one of your holidays. Just be there. Feel the warmth of the sun on your face, the gentle breeze floating lightly over your body, let the scent of the flowers drift towards you, hear the birds in the distance, see the colour of the grass. Let yourself become part of the whole scene. Just let yourself rest.

15 Imagine somewhere there is a comfortable seat. Float over to it and because you feel so relaxed you sink into the seat and fall asleep. It is a sort of dream within a dream. You will hear noises but these will not trouble you, in fact they will make you even more relaxed. Imagine that you have all the time in the world. You just let yourself experience what it is like to be fully relaxed.

16 Now imagine that all your worries and problems are floating away from you like a cloud leaving your body. You can mentally place all your worries one by one onto the cloud until it becomes heavy, thick and dark with all your problems. Then imagine this cloud leaving your body and drifting away. See it getting smaller and smaller until it disappears over the horizon. Feel what it is like to be completely free of any worry or care. Remain like this for a short while.

17 When you feel ready to come out of your relaxed state, just count: five, four, three, two, one and open your eyes. Focus on different parts of the room. Stretch yourself. Just remain like this for a few seconds and then get up and walk around the room.

Here are some points to remember:

1 The process may look complicated but after a few attempts you should be able to relax yourself quite deeply. But you must practise. Take your time. Allow things to happen. You may need to practise the earlier sections separately until you master them and then move on to the later parts of the relaxation method.

2 You can bring yourself out of your relaxation anytime you like by counting backwards: five, four, three, two, one. You need to note this and try it a few

times. Your key to becoming awake and alert is to count backwards: five, four, three, two, one. At 'one' say to yourself: 'Wide awake, completely alert!'

3 If you find it difficult to visualize, remove this section from your relaxation method. Just let your body experience what is happening.

You can make your own cassette. Use your own words to fill in the framework outlined above. Speak clearly, slowly but fairly softly. You may need to try a few attempts before you get it right.

It you use a cassette it is useful to be able to relax using the methods mentioned above without your recorder.

Here is a brief summary of the stages:

PREPARATION

   1 – make yourself relaxed

   2 – look upwards and backwards

DEEPENING

   3 – close your eyes to the count of one to five

   4 – open again, look upwards to the count of five to one

   5 – close to the count of one to five, become twice as relaxed

   6 – open to the count of five to one

   7 – close to the count of one to five, become ten times as relaxed

MENTAL RELAXATION

   8 – count backwards from 300, become mentally relaxed as you count

FURTHER DEEPENING

   9 – let yourself relax to level one

   10 – now to level two

   11 – now to the deepest level of all: level three

REMOVING STRESS

   12 – imagine yourself in a pleasant scene

   13 – see a comfortable seat, sit in it and drift away

   14 – let all your troubles disappear on a cloud

   15 – remain there for a while

WAKENING

   16 – wake yourself up by counting: five to one

This method works with most people. It has been used with managers relaxing as a group in their work place, it has helped people suffering from severe phobias and others who say that they have never been able to relax.

If you find that you are so tense when you try the exercise, you can try another method which uses your tensions to assist your relaxation, but do try the method outlined above first rather than just dabble with one method and then attempt another.

This is how it works:

Start with your left foot. Tense it and then let go. Repeat. Now your right foot. Tense and let go. Now your left ankle. Now your left leg: tense it and then let it relax. Now your right leg. Work your way through the rest of your body, tensing each part and letting go. Repeat the whole process if necessary. Then repeat again tensing and breathing out slowly to the count of five and letting go. Now start the method mentioned earlier of opening and closing your eyes.

Once you have learned to relax each day you will find yourself generally calmer. You need then to extend the process so that you can relax in specifically stress-inducing situations.

What you do is to learn to relax yourself as you count: one, two, three, four, five – breathing out slowly as you do so. Practise this quite a few times a day. Do so as you travel to work, a few times in the morning and later in the day. This will not be as deep as the fuller method but it will help you to be able to relax virtually at any time.

The last step is to become aware of what happens to you when you begin to feel stressed. To do so, either write down exactly what happens to you physically in an actual stress situation or imagine you are in that situation.

If you use imagination, really go into the situation, paint the scene vividly in your mind. Note carefully how your body responds to stress. Does your jaw tighten? Do you feel your chest becoming constricted? Or do you clench your hands? Feel hot? Does your stomach seem to turn over? Do you become hot and do you sweat? Or go quite cold? Does your neck stiffen, or your shoulders? Note these symptoms. They inform you about the start of your stress response.

Immediately you experience these sensations, you need to start counting slowly and calmly: one, two, three, four, five, breathing out gently as you do so. Repeat a few times.

Now what you need to do is to imagine circumstances which are stressful but not too threatening; count slowly and breathe out to relax yourself as the image becomes vivid to you.

See yourself mentally in a stressful situation and immediately you become aware of physical arousal – in your head, body, arms or wherever – then go through the counting and breathing procedure. You need to start counting within half a second of feeling tense. Practise until you 'pair' the physical stress symptom with the relaxation response.

You will, initially, find this difficult for really stressful conditions, so you need to start using it in minor stressful situations. After a time you will be able to apply it to more severe stressful events.

You need to use the technique along with general relaxation.

If there are many things that stress you, make a list of them and then place them in descending order of stressfulness. Write a brief description of each in the space below. Do not worry if you have less than eight in your list. If you wish,

add more than eight levels.

Your stress hierarchy:

1 The most stressful situation that occurs in your life ....

2 The second most ....

3 The third most ....

4 The fourth most ....

5 The fifth most ....

6 The sixth most ....

7 The seventh most ....

8 A situation which produces some stress which is just above the level at which you feel you can cope comfortably.

Take the least stressful situation, that is number eight in the list. Imagine yourself in it. Try to recapture it fully with all its sights, sounds, feelings, physical location, people – even your movements. Once you feel that you are into the situation and note your physical response, start to breathe out slowly to the count of five and relax yourself as you do so.

Repeat this at the same session and again later. You will eventually find that the thought of the event no longer makes you feel tense. Try doing the breathing exercise in a real situation at the same level.

Your next step is to move up your stress hierarchy, repeating the process, first in your imagination and then in an actual situation. Do not try to advance too quickly. If you find it doesn't work, move down your stress ladder a stage. Then move up again.

When you have become proficient, you should be able to use the system whenever a stress-inducing situation presents itself in real life. Always tackle things calmly and slowly.

With your general relaxation and the use of the technique for specific events you will find that because you are calmer, previously stress-inducing circumstances do not appear so powerful. You find you have time to think and to consider different ways of responding. This gives you greater control over situations.

There is another helpful exercise you can use when you find yourself ruminating, that is getting trapped into a continuous pattern of thinking negative thoughts. You can use it when your mind goes over and over old or anticipated problems, when you remind yourself about how inadequate you are, that you'll never be able to cope and what a failure you are. Say to yourself quite emphatically the word: 'STOP!' and then replace your thoughts with a positive affirmation.

To do this, list your negative thoughts. Then write down their opposites, that is a positive version of them. But do make sure your positive version is believable. Don't say: 'I have no problems', or: 'I can tackle anything'. You won't believe it.

Here are some examples of what you can say:

negative ◄————————► positive

I am useless ◄—► I can learn to cope constructively and effectively

It won't work ◄—► I can get the capacity to make it work

It is too much for me ◄—► I am gaining the capacity to be able to cope

I am a failure ◄—► I have the ability to turn myself into a success

When you find yourself ruminating, say to yourself: 'STOP!' and then emphatically make your positive statement to yourself.

Again practise. Every time you start your negative spiral, make an emphatic: 'STOP!'

Another technique you can use is imagery. Imagine yourself coping, being able to deal with situations, being a success. Flood your mind with positive images. Daydream of yourself becoming the sort of person you would like to be.

Also allow yourself to become creative, there are many ways of tackling a problem. Do not stick to the same unworkable paths.

Do not expect instant results. You must be patient with yourself. You may find that these methods work well for a while and then you meet a set-back. This is the time to persevere.

And REMEMBER:

Only YOU can help yourself. You spend years becoming technically proficient, hours deciding where to take your annual holiday and much time debating what sort of car to buy... you need to spend some hours (for that is all it takes) to tackle and remove the stress in your life. This book, the cassette plus your own efforts will help you become a more efficient and less stressful person.

These relaxation methods are common to all sorts of stress. They should be used in combination with examining the pattern of stressors in your life so that you advance on two fronts – becoming more calm and removing causes.

Much stress is connected with work. The next chapter explores the techniques that you have already used but in more depth and related to your job. You should find that you are becoming more and more skilled at analysing stress patterns and should find it easy to work through the exercises in the next chapter.

TOPIC REFERENCES

Chemically induced emotions:
Schachter, S., in *Cognitive theories in social psychology*, (Berkowski, 'Interactions of cognitive and psychological determinants of emotional state' ed.), Academic Press, 1978.

Stress and allergies:
Rippere, V., *The allergy problem.* Thorsons, 1983.

Relaxation:
Benson, H., *The relaxation response.* Avon, 1975.

Coe, W. C., 'Hypnosis and suggestion in behavioural change', in *Helping people change.* Pergamon, 1980.
Garmany, G., *Muscle relaxation,* Actinic Press, 1952.
Wolpe, J., *Psychotherapy by reciprocal inhibition.* Stanford University Press, 1958.

Thought stopping:
Rimm, D. C., 'Thought stopping and covert assertion in the treatment of phobias', in *Journal of clinical psychology,* vol. 41. BPS, 1973.

PART TWO

STRESS AND WORK

CHAPTER 5

Stress themes and work

You spend about forty hours of each week at work. Something like two hundred days a year are allocated to your working life. This major influence on how you live can create tensions of many different kinds. The way you perceive your responsibilities; work relationships; plus the actual tasks – their quantity, quality demanded and complexity may be major contributors to stress in your life.

Stress may be all too clear to you. It could however be hidden; you may find yourself with an undercurrent of tension because you are not doing what you really want to do, missing for you is daily satisfaction and fulfilment. Your job does not demand much effort, is not difficult and physical conditions are fine – but you are bored.

For others, the problem is different: physical conditions produce strain. Some find the conflict between the urgent demands of work and pressures at home induce problems which lead to stress.

You may find your problem centred around being 'blocked in', being unable to see any future development in your chosen career.

Or perhaps it is that you are not clear about what is expected of you. Alternatively, the difficulties may be centred around having to attempt to meet conflicting demands.

To tackle stress in your work life, you need to pinpoint specific stressors as you have done with stress in other parts of your life. These insights direct your energies into tackling the basis of your problem.

CHRONIC AND ACUTE STRESS

As with your home life and other activities, stress can be chronic. It is not dramatic, nor intensely painful but a dull, continuous dissatisfaction which has been your companion for years. You tolerate it.

For others, stress is acute – even dramatic and frightening. You've lost your job, and you don't know how you are going to manage. You feel you will never work again at your age. For years you have extended your skills, worked loyally and sacrificed your leisure time. Now all this is finished.

Stress may be bedded in some event in the past which still has power over you, or it could be directly connected with your present daily work. You are living it at the moment. You faced it yesterday, today and will for the rest of this week – and you feel that you daren't look any further.

Stress is not only connected with past and present conditions. It can be anticipatory about real or imagined situations. You expect something to happen which is threatening. What it is may not be all that clear. Uncertainty increases its power. Although nothing has happened yet, your present life is affected.

SUMMARIZING – stress can be:

> acute
> or chronic
> > connected with present day events
> > anticipatory
> > related to the past.

WORK STRESS AND YOU

This chapter reviews some of the main causes of work-related stress. Your own stress patterns may correspond to some of these but the exact reason for your problems is likely to be complex and range over a wide area. Causes are likely to interact with each other, adding to your burden. You will need, therefore, to pinpoint your specific difficulties and what is behind them.

Where stress is chronic and connected with present day activities, you may be able to tackle it partly by improving your work skills. This does not help with anticipatory or retrospectively caused stress. If you failed in an important work assignment last year, improving your present day skills won't alter the past. Tackling chronic daily stressors requires a different approach from dealing with an acute major issue.

Later you can start to compile your personal stress profile. As with your previous work on more general stress in your life, some of your job stressors are likely to be part of larger meta-themes with minor ones connected to them.

Dealing with these meta-themes is more valuable than concentrating on less important issues. If you feel that your career is at a dead end, it is not so fruitful to use your energies to tackle minor problems you are experiencing with your secretary over her way of arriving late each week day.

META-THEMES

Your whole concept of work itself, the meaning you give to what you do with your work life and how you see it in relation to the rest of your life, provides an important framework which fashions how you live. If there is something wrong with this framework, tinkering with smaller aspects is ineffective.

As a start to looking at what work means to you, complete the following sentence, giving three different answers:

work to me means......
Write these down:

answer number 1.................

answer number 2.................

answer number 3.................

Close your eyes and let your imagination wander as think of your work. What images emerged? Were they bright? Dull? Clear? Fuzzy? Was there a theme? Try to capture the feelings that arose as you visualized your work. Excitement? Fear? Hostility?

You may have written things like:

1 A way of earning a living.
2 Something unpleasant I have to put up with.
3 An exciting, rewarding experience.
4 Being exploited.
5 Something that makes me tired and irritable on a Monday.
6 An important means of self-development.

7 Something I do each work day which is not really important to me.

When you closed your eyes, you may have seen in your mind's eye a conflict, a mass of work being imposed on you, some exciting scene, a dull factory gate on a wet Monday in winter and so on.

Stay with your images for a moment. Ask yourself what do they mean. Just listen to yourself talking about your work.

What emerges provides a clue about your work meta-theme.

Let's look at the examples given above. The first one suggests seeing work as a means to an end. You work to earn so that you can survive and to support your lifestyle.

The second answer indicates that work gets in the way of your real life; it certainly does not add any pleasure to it.

The third represents work as an important influence in your life. Much of your life energy is expended in furthering your career. You get satisfaction from making the grade.

Now take a deeper look at what you have written. Consider the opposites to your answers (remember that your answers may be quite different from the example below):

1 Earning a living ←→ going without.
2 Unpleasant experience ←→ enjoying myself.
3 Fulfilment ←→ depression.
4 Being exploited ←→ co-operation.
5 Dreading the week ahead ←——→ looking forward to it.
6 Personal growth ←→ stagnation.
7 Not especially important ←——→ important to me.

C. Brooklyn Derr of the University of Utah, USA, has proposed five orientations about work. Not everyone he suggests wants to advance to the top of her or his profession.

Derr's list included: getting ahead, getting secure, getting free, getting high and the final one: getting balanced.

Most of these are self-explanatory. Getting free is concerned with personal autonomy, not being confined by the demands of work organizations and role norms. Getting high is about the need for excitement, action and commitment in a job.

Other research, especially in sociology, suggests that many of us do not work because of the job itself but just as a means of earning money. Satisfactions are realized outside the job. Taking this approach, that of Derr and from many discussions with people about how they see work, eight major themes emerge. These need to be empirically tested but at present they are a convenient way of classifying what work tends to mean to most people.

You are likely to find that you fit more than one meta-theme. You may find one or two more important, or you may feel that your choices conflict with each other.

These major themes are:

1 CAREER – work as a career where success is important.
2 INSTRUMENTAL – a way of earning money to buy things which make life satisfying.
3 SECURITY – to provide basic security in life.
4 VOCATION – expressing your talents and aptitudes.
5 DOING YOUR OWN THING – a way of self-development and liberation.
6 BALANCE – one part of life to be balanced with other aspects.
7 TAKING WHAT COMES – just accepting what's available, either as a positive choice or you feel that this is how it has to be.

8 POLITICAL – seeing work as a political issue.

Each theme has within it the possibility of generating stress.

Moving from one orientation to another is also stressful. If you have dedicated yourself to a successful career and then try to downgrade work to seek balance with your home life, wife and children, you may feel stressed as the pressures from work continue to press their demands on you; or that your family does not respond positively to your new interests in them. They have learned to live without you and now, from their point of view, you are intruding into their lives.

Another problem is when your partner does not share your attitude to work. You clash because your priorities differ. You see things differently, as you operate in dissimilar worlds. For you a career is number one priority, your partner feels that home and family are equally important.

William devoted his life to work. He remained there late in the evening and saw little of his children. His leisure was used to further his job. To William, home and wife were a resource – useful for entertaining clients. Home was also a place where *he* could recuperate and recharge his batteries to emerge refreshed for further intense work activity.

Mary, his wife, felt William was unfair to her and to the children. Both Mary and William were tense, dissatisfied and angry. The stress created by William's demanding job was further intensified by friction at home as he and his wife clashed over what was important in their lives.

Let's look at some of these meta-themes and see how they can lead to stress.

1 Career . . .

You seek promotion, status and power. You value financial rewards. You are competitive. You are committed, energetic and work to win. Your home life takes second place. You live where the company suggests. You move when the company changes your territory. They want the right person in the right place at the right time. You do not question the assumption that they should dictate which part of the country or indeed the world in which you are to live. And anyway, you have heard of the few who failed to respond. They didn't get far in the company.

You present to the world the right image of the sort of person you feel the company wishes you to be. Your tastes, hobbies and leisure activities are fashioned by company considerations.

Fine, if this is what you want and excellent if you can afford your chosen lifestyle. But playing golf if you don't like it, entertaining people you'd rather not be with, sending your children to a private school when you can hardly afford it, purchasing a car to impress, moving to a house in the 'right' area but with a crippling mortgage and playing a role which represses important parts of your real self provides the elements for a stressful life.

You may also find yourself trapped as you have to continue along your chosen path by having to meet financial obligations to which you are committed. You find yourself forced to continue to put an intensity into your work to even remain where you are. Over your shoulder you can see others pursuing the same path and at any time ready to overtake you.

If you are a type A personality, you have an inner need to be competitive, tough, and you delight in working under pressure. You like challenge and uncertainty. With this pressure, you'll almost certainly suffer some stress even though you feel you are enjoying yourself. Another problem is that your dynamic approach may not always be the most effective. When things don't go well, you'll tend to intensify your present management style, putting even more effort into pushing things along. You may lack flexibility and the capacity to use less obvious styles of management.

The career-orientated executive or professional spends limited time with the family. At home you're frequently too tired to be much of a parent. A recent survey showed that many senior managers were too exhausted because of their job pressures even to have sex with their wives!

Business favours this lifestyle. You'll model yourself on older and successful managers. Providing you do not threaten them, they will support you. You are the sort of person the organization needs. You'll find your behaviour is reinforced. You'll be rated highly at your annual appraisal. Try getting out of that!

Type A personality is a global description for competitive, thrusting, impatient and aggressive personalities.

Type Bs are placid, taking things as they come. Many of us are in the middle.

Type As are twice as likely to suffer heart attacks compared with Type Bs. Only some aspects, however, of Type A behaviour are harmful. The danger comes from hostile, angry, and untrusting traits not just from being competitive, driving and dynamic itself. It doesn't matter whether the anger finds expression as outward rage or whether it remains trapped within you. The result is the same: the likelihood of heart problems. The hostility part of Type A behaviour is a good predictor of blocked arteries and death from heart disease. Blood pressure may not be generally

enhanced but such behaviours trigger surges of increased pressure and this is where the danger lies.

Getting nowhere

Within the theme of work as a career can arise the feeling that after some years, progress seems to cease. We sense we are getting nowhere.

This can be a particular problem for some graduates. They get their first job and bring into their chosen firm specialized skills and a keen mind.

The firm helps them develop these and related skills in the area of their specialism. Their knowledge deepens. They become more and more expert in a narrowing field related to the practicalities of their jobs. The years go by, they become older and they are eventually promoted and become middle managers. Financial rewards are good.

But where now? Skills are not really suitable for other posts at the same level in the firm. The salary is too high for them to retrain and start afresh in a new area. Upward promotion is limited. They have reached their peak. They can't move up, out or sideways. Their very proficiency is their failure. They are boxed in; locked in by success. Yesterday's excitements have faded. There is little scope to modify the present job. It is done effectively already.

A Canadian study showed that the sort of people who become locked in are older managers who have been with their company longer than their peers. They are more passive, conservative, submissive, dependent and less skilled in handling people. Results: feeling dissatisfied, worthless and stressful. They also suffer more physical illnesses. It is not certain whether the conservatism and dependency is the cause or the result of their predicament. The study shows that these qualities differentiate managers who feel, and are, trapped from those who do not.

It is not that every manager, or even the majority, are locked in. Some make certain that they move into different departments to broaden their experience.

Other managers, even though they remain in the same department, ensure that they actively relate their efforts to the wider interests of the company. They do not exist in the tight little world of their own department. They are proactive, not just reacting to circumstances. They take the initiative. They push themselves and their departments. They try to keep one step ahead of events. They are innovative, not just waiting for new ideas to be imposed on them. They stand up, fight back, know when to compromise and are skilled in handling people at all levels.

Some organizations make certain their executives do not fall into the 'boxed-in, nowhere-to-go' trap.

The real answer to stress created by feeling that you have reached your limit in your department, cannot move out but still have untapped potential, is not to let it happen!

You might, in your imagination, work out a number of possible scenarios about where your work path is likely to lead you. You can then ask yourself how you would feel in such situations. If your projections are not what you want, your next task is to decide how you can avoid those pathways from unfolding. Then take steps to actively change course. Animals learn from experience but what they cannot do (as far as we know) is to anticipate the future and learn from what might have happened.

To learn from imaginary futures is safe and provides experiences without actually living through them. The capacity to learn from imaginary experiences is a valuable asset. Take advantage of it.

In the UK another study of graduate managers showed an initial motivation when first joining their new company of wanting to get things done, to exercise power and a desire to turn plans and ideas into practical realities.

Most get married, have children and the pressures of family demands begin to force a change in priorities. Ambition is weakened and the pace slackens. By the mid-thirties, these executives begin to look back and realize how little they have achieved of their early ambitions. More importantly, they sense that time is running out. Some accept this and attempt to maintain a balance between the conflicting demands of work and family. Others put everything they've got into their work to make up for lost time. Home, family, leisure, all take second place. It is now or never. They feel they may not make it. This provides a sort of desperation to get results and prove that they are what they once thought they were.

If you feel these ideas fit your style, you find yourself pushing harder, becoming more aggressive, competitive and dominating. You compete with others like yourself. You may find yourself working for a boss who feels the same as you, or one who gets in your way. You mentally and emotionally cut yourself off from your family as priorities change. There is stress both from pushing and succeeding and from failing to make the grade, as well as marriage problems.

The way out is to realize what is happening, search within yourself to find out what you really want out of your life and discuss matters openly with your partner. You may need to examine why you feel that your worth as a person is solely bound up with being, and being seen to be, a success at work. The solution may not be to throw it all in but to rebalance your life so that other needs are met. Study how many people have made a success of their work life without being aggressive, competitive and ruthless.

Not everyone takes this path of 'now or never'; some of us accept the way things have turned out. We are no longer so dedicated to work. Making our targets becomes an effort. We become more concerned with social and self-esteem needs. Our health assumes greater importance. We may feel jealous when we are passed over for promotion but secretly we are relieved. We didn't really want the responsibility. Our present level suits us. Our concern is to survive in what we are doing by ensuring that we give the minimum necessary to get by.

There are degrees of acceptance of a declining upward career path. Some of us provide a fair – if far from spectacular, return for our salaries. Others only look interested and play a game of appearing to do a good job of work. Attending meetings, producing reports, motivating their staff and looking as if they are performing as successful mid-career managers. It is all much of a sham. Whilst they appear keen, they resent change, withhold information, avoid responsibility and hand problems to others. Some are very skilled at looking efficient but doing little. The problem is that at the back of their minds is the hidden worry that someone will call their bluff or that the department will be reorganized, or that they'll get a new boss and have to start working again!

As the years go by, priorities tend to change again. By the mid-forties or so, we've either made the grade or missed it (at least for most of us).

If we feel we've reached what we set out to achieve we rearrange our priorities. We don't have to fight any longer. Social and family concerns begin to assume greater importance. (We may have remarried by this time.)

If we set out to win and failed, we may feel the frustration and depression of a life wasted.

These concepts of career patterns are painted in black and white to highlight the key factors. They are what Weber called 'idealized' descriptions – key elements are extracted. It is likely that you will relate only to certain limited aspects. The aim is to start you thinking about how you see work and your career lifestyle and for you to realize that others have trodden a similar path. This helps us to understand that we share similar conflicts and dilemmas with others. Seeing how stress relates to wider issues of career themes can be a first step to changing things. It helps us to explore deeper issues instead of tinkering with trivia.

Life and career

Career patterns are part of a wider series of stepping stones through a lifetime. There are a couple of other theories worth examining because they might provide insight into where you are and where you want to go. One is Maslow's theory of self-actualization. The theory is speculative. It is not backed up by empirical evidence but it does open up avenues worth exploring. It is presented for this reason. If you feel it relates to your situation, examine the meaning it has in your life. Use it as a starting point to consider what satisfaction you have, need and miss in your work.

According to Maslow, humans have a hierarchy of needs. These range from basic needs to higher level ones concerned with self-actualization. Once a lower need has been met, we then seek the next higher level one. Built into this concept is the idea of continuous dissatisfaction. We seek to reach a goal and as soon as we succeed, a new dissatisfaction makes itself felt and pushes us further upwards. Dissatisfaction itself need not be negative, it is the motive power which drives us on to these higher and more fulfilling goals in our lives.

Maslow postulates a five-level hierarchy, starting with basic concerns about safety and ending with self-actualization.

If survival and safety are threatened, we are not concerned with the richer things of life; nothing matters except to be alive tomorrow. Once we feel reasonably safe and secure, however, we have an inner feeling that life surely must be more than this. Safety is insufficient for a satisfied life. We expect more.

Demands for socially orientated satisfaction take over our energies. We ask to be accepted, have friends and be loved. Many, who do not feel that they are part of any group, think of nothing else other than what they must do to become accepted. For others, feeling that we are part of society through our family, groups of friends, working colleagues and others, becomes almost unnoticed. It seems so natural and usual that we are not aware that this is part of our lives. The only time it becomes obvious is when we are rejected or move to a new town and find ourselves friendless. Then we realize the value of our former friendships. Being socially accepted still leaves a feeling that something is missing. Maslow suggests that what we then seek is self-esteem – a firmly based evaluation of ourselves by others.

If we are lucky enough to realize this need, we begin to strive for independence – to control our own lives, do our own thing, to be autonomous.

At the top of the hierarchy is self-actualization. To be self-actualized is to be 'a full person, to forget our poses, defences and shyness, to experience life fully and vividly'.

Maslow writes of such people transcending time, culture, the past, ego, the rat race – even evil, pain and discomfort. Each day presents a series of choices: the self-actualized person makes the positive choice – not necessarily the easy one.

Within this framework are dissatisfactions which push us on to more meaningful lives. There is a discontent about humankind that is the source of our striving – not to overcome disabilities but to attain deeper meanings and satisfactions. Stress may be related to not achieving what we feel is potentially for us. Our present satisfactions are insufficient.

At a recent seminar I ran for people who wanted to change their lives, there were two distinct groups. There were those who had recently been through a painful experience which had removed from their lives, through a break up of a marriage or death of a partner, some pretty important basic needs. There were others whose lives seemed, on the face of it, reasonably good but felt that there was something missing. The first group sought to reclaim something important that had been taken away. The second group sought independence, with one or two asking for a quality in their lives which very much resembled Maslow's self-actualization.

Not so much a hierarchy more a . . .
Whilst there is little empirical evidence for five discrete levels of needs, other researchers have found that people (at least within certain cultures) do have clusters of human necessities similar to those suggested by Maslow.

Alderfer in the United States found that three categories seem to emerge:

1 Existence.
2 Relatedness.
3 Growth.

These are similar to Maslow's but they do not form a simple hierarchy. We do not necessarily move from lower to higher levels. One, two or even three needs may operate at the same time – each with varying intensity. If satisfaction in one area is denied, we continue to persist along that route but also regress by putting more effort into lower needs. Our growth needs are stunted but we still push for some development towards our goals, whilst putting more and more energy into making friends and socializing. Those of us who do not feel so secure spend much of our time, money and thought in ensuring that we do not take risks. We play safe, take out large insurance cover and are cautious about our health. We are not satisfied but it is too risky to move out. We are stuck with our dissatisfactions.

Needs can be chronic, persisting over a long time or temporary, altering with changing situations.

This is a more complex picture and means that simple motivation theories of what people want out of work are insufficient. People's needs change. They ask for a mixture that meets their present-day personal requirements. At a number of management seminars I've run, participants have taken a simple test to establish their needs. Results: *always* a wide range. Some asked for basic satisfactions, others concentrated on social needs and some on self-actualization. Most stated that what they wanted was a mixture of varying strengths.

A wider view still . . .
One further theory might help you to locate your present position in your lifetime. Erik Erikson, mentioned in an earlier chapter, extended Freud's ideas of childhood development. From his clinical work he suggested that there are a number of stages we face as we develop from baby to child, and from child to adolescent and then into adulthood. Again the evidence lacks empirical backing but it does offer categories which provide a means of starting to see our present dilemmas in a wider context.

Each stage, according to Erikson, presents a crisis within which is a direction to travel with positive or negative outcomes.

In the first few months of life we acquire *basic trust* or *mistrust* which remains as a psychic undercurrent during the remainder of our lives.

This provides the foundation on which is built the way we feel about trusting others. Basic trust helps us in taking risks in making relationships. It helps us to be able to be close to others; or it cuts us off from ever fully trusting another. This early relationship, according to Erikson, colours the way we see our world – for good or ill. Of course, there are degrees of trust and some of us just need a lot of reassurance before we place our trust in another. We are aware of our vulnerability.

The next stage follows from, and is based upon, our first early crisis of trust or mistrust. The second stage offers a choice between *autonomy* or *shame*. Whichever way it turns out, it again affects subsequent development.

Then follows a crisis of *initiative* v *guilt*; where, if successful we assert ourselves on our immediate environment and channel our urges into socially acceptable ways.

The next is *industry* v *inferiority*. We learn to learn and begin to feel more and more competent in our world; or we see ourselves as failures.

The next move is to early adolescence with a crisis of *identity* v *role confusion*. We learn who we are. In some cultures this stage is ritualized. There are ceremonies which transform us from a child into a man or woman. In the West, the changeover is less clear. It is a time of experiment, of doubt and of some confusion. We try out different identities, passing through periods of being a punk, a rebel and so on until we find a personality which seems to fit us. A strong self-concept emerges if we are successful; or if not, we remain confused about our true identity. This lack hinders future development.

We move then onto a stage concerned with a dilemma of *intimacy* v *isolation*. Having 'found' our real self, we now 'find' another, with whom to share our lives. Failing this means to experience deep isolation.

The next stage is called *generativity* v *stagnation*. We need to be productive, creative, to feel that we are contributing to our world. The alternative is to stagnate. You may see the link with the earlier examples of mid-career crises.

As a starting point look back over your life and see how these crises applied to you, how successfully you passed through them and, if you did not, how they might have affected your life. You might feel, for instance, that you lack basic trust and can never fully commit yourself to another person; that you always have to hold back something of yourself; that you are never quite certain about who you are and what you want to do with your life and that you feel your contribution to your part of the world generates very little of value.

Whilst these clinical insights lack true scientific evidence, they do provide a feeling of how some events have fashioned who we are.

The final crisis is one of *integrity* v *despair*. Maybe we sense that at the end we will sum it all up and feel that we have lived a worthwhile life; or that we have missed the boat and do not have any more time or another life time to try again.

These landmarks help us chart where we are and where we might be heading. they take us away from immediate issues and provide a sense of perspective as we compare our journey with those who have passed before.

Your route may be different. Your life stages may not be so distinct. Crisis points may be faced earlier – perhaps when you are not ready for them. A client of mine spent eleven years of her life in hospital and at sixteen found it difficult to relate to others of her own age. She learned about suffering and death, the uncertainy and fragility of life but little about how to mix with others. She had to face issues which needed an older and more mature mind. Issues which were relevant to her age she could not experience because circumstances made it impossible. She was out of phase with life.

Crisis points are stressful. They cannot be otherwise. But they also present opportunities. They can be growth points.

Being career orientated presents the possibility of an exciting life full of satisfaction for some, for others it is the major cause of their stress. By considering some of these points, you may begin to see more clearly a pathway out of your problems.

2 I'm here only for the money...

The second attitude to work already mentioned briefly is what is called an instrumental one; work is an instrument to obtain other things. The job itself is not important. What is important is the money you earn. Through spending, you purchase goods that make life interesting. Your purchases make a statement about who you are. Others, you feel, are able to see the sort of person you are from your lifestyle. A career as such is not important except that it enhances your pay.

If your job is boring then the daily work grind is something to be got through as quickly as possible. Real living begins when you leave the office or factory gate. Work is just a means to an end. You'll even take less satisfying work for greater financial reward. Your interests are in your home, hobbies, holidays, social activities and especially your possessions.

You judge people by what they own – the car they drive, the sort of house they live in and how they furnish it. You assume they assess you in the same way.

Studies of the so-called affluent working class suggest that many skilled and semi-skilled workers belong to this category. They are described as 'privatized' persons who have little social contact with their fellow workers, other than about the job itself.

Stress affects such people in a number of ways. First through the job itself; it may be uninteresting, physically demanding and offer little or no control over what is done, when and how it is performed. Only limited contact may be possible with fellow workers. Some years ago, I did a number of surveys of workers who spent hours moving pieces of metal around, performing a set of operations and then repeating the cycle every few minutes. The work was arranged so that, although they were close to each other, they could not talk easily together. They did this, day in and day out, hour after hour; some for many years. Others had become dulled to their job but there was an undercurrent of tension.

Distasteful as the job may be, when it is threatened because of possible reorganization, changes in work methods through the introduction of new technology or, worst of all, because of threatened closure, stress becomes severe. The job may have been hated but it did provide the means to get what you wanted from life. Something important is threatened. Redundancy, you feel, will destroy your lifestyle.

Even if your job is not threatened, you feel you need to keep your income rising so that you keep ahead in the money stakes. Harsh economic conditions make this impossible and you feel this is unfair and blame your firm.

3 Working to make it safe . . .

The major orientation here is not working for a career, for promotion, for success, or for power. Neither do you work for money. What is important for you is security.

Security provides a basis on which stands the rest of your life. Threaten your security and your stress is evident. You select a firm and a job which offers certainty. You play safe. You do not stick your neck out. In return you offer your firm, your manager and your department loyalty. You expect to be rewarded for time served and for your commitment to be valued.

You expect a reasonable salary but you'd never press for more. You do not see yourself as part of the rat race.

Stress for you occurs when your expectations are shattered; when your firm no longer appreciates loyalty and long service. Your whole idea of what work is about seems no longer valid. You may continue to act as if it were and attempt to keep tension, stress and worry from surfacing. You try to remain in the cosy world of yesterday. Underneath it all you realize that you were only a number on a payroll. Alternatively, you may accept the new reality and the overt strain that goes with it but at least get on with doing something about it.

Redundancy is even more stressful. You realize the years you have given the firm are not really valued. Your view of what the world is supposed to be about is smashed. With it, you as a person are shattered. Your stress is both chronic and acute.

Having a job gives you an identity. 'And what do you do?' people ask. 'Nothing', you have to reply. . .

4 A sense of vocation . . .

The fourth way is to view work as a vocation; working because it satisfies something within you. There is excitement, action and enjoyment in doing what you really like doing. Sports persons, performers, musicians, circus folk and entertainers may work for the joy of the actual activity of their work.

Entrepreneurs who wrap themselves up totally in fashioning and running their own organizations, generating ideas and turning these into realities are also in this category. These are the self-actualizers, ranging from artists who have a feeling for what can be expressed in oils and the talent to execute it. Included also are those devoted to a particular cause – political, religious, looking after donkeys, running a hospice or fighting against real or imagined injustices.

Intense involvement is the key. Work is living. What is done is the purpose of existence. Such commitment makes it difficult to cut yourself off from work activities. Everything is subordinated to what you feel you must do. There are, of course, degrees of intensity from the total commitment of a saint to that of an entrepreneur who can at times detach him or herself.

Intensity generates stress. This is felt when we pause. We realize how tired we have become. It is physically and mentally draining to be a person who does not easily give up. One such person said to me that he did not realize the pressures until he had to stop because of his urgent need for a heart by-pass operation.

Another source of stress is failure. We have not just let ourselves down but also the cause to which we are devoted.

Stress too, is connected with attempting to reconcile work activities with family demands. These are subordinated to the prime task of work. Family members perceive things differently. Our children may feel that we do not care enough about them.

A further cause of stress is that other demands of life stop us doing what we feel we should do. Our hopes remain unfulfilled dreams; economic conditions force us to remain amateur painters or musicians. We go through life half-heartedly knowing that we will not do with it what we wished to do.

Stress also arises when we become disillusioned. We realize the deficiencies of what we have devoted our lives to. The massive reconstruing of core values threatens our view of ourselves. It applies to scientists whose reputation is built upon certain theories; to ministers of religion who begin to doubt the validity of their faith; to political activitists who move from a simplistic, black and white way of seeing things to a complexity which matches the world as it is more realistically.

We now see that our enemies might have been right. The world knows us as a convinced person with strong, clear, definite views. We have fought for them. We have been seen as committed. We have condemned others for standing on the sidelines. Now we face the condemnation of others who feel that we have betrayed them. And we have to do something with the rest of our lives.

5 Doing your own thing . . .

Another orientation is to use work as a means of self-development and personal fulfilment. Whereas with work as a sense of vocation, your satisfaction comes from devoting what you do to a cause; with personal development, you spend your energies extending your skills, experience, interests and making full use of whatever talents and inclinations you possess. To achieve this, you must be free to do what needs to be done and to cease doing so when necessary.

You do not fit the normal work mould. A career must not impose its standards and demands on your life. You are not concerned with moving upwards but with personal autonomy. You value independence, personal space and control over your life.

Your work pattern involves change. Other people in your life may fail to see a pattern or make any sense of what you do as you move out of what you are doing into new, and for you necessary, experiences which are important for your personal development.

Some find you superficial. You seem to them to exist on the margin of things. You are in the organization but not of it. Your commitment is not to the ethos of the firm that employs you; it is to your own concept of how your current activities fit into your life/work plan.

Stress can result from a number of factors: not getting what you want means stagnation and this is your most important stressor; the need for personal space creates a distance between yourselves and others, so you do not have such close personal contact; daily pressures of the job may stifle what you want to do as your needs clash with those of the organization.

Your family seek security, a better standard of living and for you to spend more time with them. They ask that you stay with the known rather than risk moving into uncertain pathways. They resent the disruption as they learn that they are all moving home once again.

There are the pressures from powerful socialization processes to fit into the expected career pattern. Your parents, friends and school teachers remind you of the importance of a career and not just playing around with life. You get a strong message to settle down.

And there are the temptations to accept a well-paid job, lured by the prospects of security and extra spending power. You see examples in the independent consultant who gets sucked into the power network of the organization, the freelance writer who takes a staff job, the ethnographer who forsakes his marginality, goes native or places his loyalties with dominant parts of the community he is studying.

Stress is also connected with loneliness of being on the margin of society, of sacrificing a sense of belonging and of fitting in with what others expect.

Stress may also be severe if you do not respond to your inner compulsion to use your life to express what capacities and talents you possess.

6 Trying to fit it all in . . .

Another way to conceptualize work is to see it as just one part of life; other parts are equally important. You seek balance, trying to reconcile job demands with those of your home, your own self-development and leisure needs.

You can do this superficially, allocating so many hours to work, so many to the children, to cultural pursuits and so on. You try to be fair to all – even to yourself. But you don't seem to please anybody. Sharing time and resources results in deficiencies all round – family members expect each other to meet *their* emotional needs, at times these needs are bound to clash. Others feel that you have failed them because you are not supporting them when they need you.

You can try at a deeper level. Hours are not balanced or allocated 'fairly' but according to some more meaningful priority system. Your daughter needs considerable support as she prepares for her exam, your son wants to be left alone, your partner wants help as she or he faces a difficult crisis. So you attempt to provide what is needed.

This is not a straightforward option. You work from carefully thought out priorities but your partner may not share these or even see them as fair. Pressures change. Your job demands you work late but your family wants your time. You would like to walk in the mountains but the lawn needs cutting. You would prefer to study another language but need to concentrate on cost accounting because that's one of the weaknesses mentioned in your last appraisal. You end up with compromise.

7 Taking what comes . . .

Another, but not so commonly admitted, meta-theme is to take what comes. This can be an active choice or because you feel that is how it has to be.

To let things happen can mean getting what you don't like. It can fashion a sense of purposelessness. Family, friends, career officers and others remind you that you need to try harder and make up your mind where you want to go with your life. The message you get from them is that you are a failure. You may begin to doubt yourself and be sucked into their perception of what you should do. On the other hand, there can be a sense of relief as you don't bother too much about what sort of work you do. You take what's around and get on with the rest of your life.

8 Work as a political issue...

For some, work itself is seen as a potential source of conflict because of the prevailing political and social set up. This is mainly a Marxist or neo-Marxist viewpoint. Those who are not owners of the means of production (or their agents) are exploited. This alienates them, that is cuts them off from their true nature, from work itself, from the product of their labours and from their fellow workers.

It is impossible to prove or disprove the validity of such beliefs. In Marxist terms world history shows, in its unfolding, the development of such exploitation reaching a stage as we have in the present world where two major forces confront each other: the exploited proletariat and the exploiting bourgeoisie. In the end the proletariat will dominate and eventually, after a period of dictatorship by the proletariat, true communism will reign and people will be set free.

There is no doubt that workers have been and are exploited. Whether a proletarian revolution would improve things is another matter. Alienation is a different concept from stress but it is likely that people who feel alienated will also be stressed. In a study I did, I found that whilst the majority of subjects in a sample of over two thousand were dissatisfied, their dissatisfaction was not statistically significantly linked with any major social factor such as occupation, class, income, housing conditions etc. It is unlikely that alienation would exist without dissatisfaction so the link with social causes was not supported.

Whether the Marxist philosophy is true or not is not the point as far as this book is concerned. What is relevant is that if you believe that it is so, then you act within the framework of your beliefs. You fight what you believe is an unjust system. This may make your main task not your job but your battle for your cause. Stress is related to the points mentioned earlier about a sense of vocation. The meaning of your life is tied up with political battle. Failure to convince others, and later possible disillusionment, may be stressful.

PUTTING IT TOGETHER . . .

Each meta-theme contains the seeds of possible stress. Your career may turn out as you wish, you find a secure job, you receive enough money to do what you want to do or you are happy with taking what turns up and have been lucky so far. This is fine. There may be some stress but it is tolerable and possibly even healthy. Your work provides sufficient satisfaction.

Within each theme, however, there are potential problems. Stress also results from conflicts *between* the different work orientations.

You can take any two and see potential conflict:

career *v* just allowing things to happen

career *v* playing safe

career *v* freedom

career *v* following our own satisfaction

career *v* seeking balance

freedom *v* playing safe

freedom *v* seeking balance

seeking balance *v* following our own needs

and so on.

Choice always involves some loss. You have insufficient resources to direct your energies into too many channels.

A way of looking at your meta-needs is to see how much importance you place on each of them.

Fill in, by grading, what priority and what importance you feel you place on each of the main categories. Remember that each category has a special meaning which has been explained earlier. Read through the discussion again so that you are clear about what you are assessing.

YOUR OWN PRESENT PRIORITIES

(As they are, not as you would like them to be)

career
instrumental
security
satisfaction
self-development
balance
take what comes

The scale is from one to five:

1 Not important at all.
2 Not so important.
3 Fairly neutral.
4 Of some importance.
5 Important.

Do not show your chart to your partner but ask her/him to complete a similar one about how he/she thinks you see your priorities.

YOUR PARTNER'S ASSESS-MENT OF HOW HE/SHE THINKS YOU SEE WORK

career
instrumental
security
satisfaction
self-development
balance
take what comes

Use the same scale.
Now repeat the exercise about how you would like things to be.

YOUR PREFERRED PRIORITIES

career
instrumental
security
satisfaction
self-development
balance
take what comes

YOUR PARTNER'S DESIRED WORK ORIENTATION FOR YOU

career
instrumental
security
satisfaction
self-development
balance
take what comes

If both of you work, then your partner can repeat the exercise.

When you have both completed the exercise, discuss it together.

Consider the difference in points allocation. Note:

1 Whether you both see things the same way.

2 How well your present priorities mesh with what you'd ideally like them to be.

3 If you both work, how similar or different are your priorities about work?

You may see clearly that you are where you both want to be but this is rare. Conflict may be fundamental because you deeply desire one orientation and are trapped in a very different one. Another possibility is that your partner sees things differently from you or that he/she assumed that your priorities were other than what they are.

Although this may seem a somewhat depressing exercise, it can be liberating. It can free you from construing work only in one way. It helps you to examine options and brings inter-family conflict into the open enabling you to discuss and perhaps resolve previously suppressed differences.

Stress in your life may be connected with such major issues rather than specific on-the-job frictions. You may find, however, that you have invested them with considerable power but that they are in fact only a displacement for more important issues. Your stress may seem to be about getting your work out on time but underneath it all you don't really care – you would rather be elsewhere.

STRESS WITHIN THE JOB . . .

You have examined major issues connected with your work lifestyle. You now need to look at factors within the job itself and at organizational structures inside your firm to see whether they induce or add to stress in your life.

You may be successfully career orientated but still find some aspects of your job stressful. You certainly do not want to sacrifice your chosen and generally rewarding career to reduce stress but you do want to make life easier for yourself.

Another important area to look at is the interrelationship between home and work. Work and home-life cannot be easily separated.

LOOKING AT WHERE YOU ARE . . .

To capture your personal feelings about what you've just read, you can work through a repertory grid. You do so in the same way as you did in earlier parts of this book.

Here are the elements:

1 Your present work.
2 Ideal work.
3 Likely future work.
4 Home life now.
5 Ideal home life.
6 Likely future home life.
7 Self-development activity now.
8 Ideal self-development activity.
9 Likely self-development activity.

Select elements as you've done previously and place them in the grid in figure 19.

Select elements in this order:

1	1, 2, and 3
2	4, 5 and 6
3	7, 8 and 9
4	1, 4 and 7
5	2, 5 and 8
6	3, 6 and 9
7	1, 5, and 9
8	2, 3 and 4
9	6, 7 and 8

If you have worked through the previous exercises you should have, by now, become quite proficient in doing grids. The main procedures will be repeated briefly here, but if you are in any

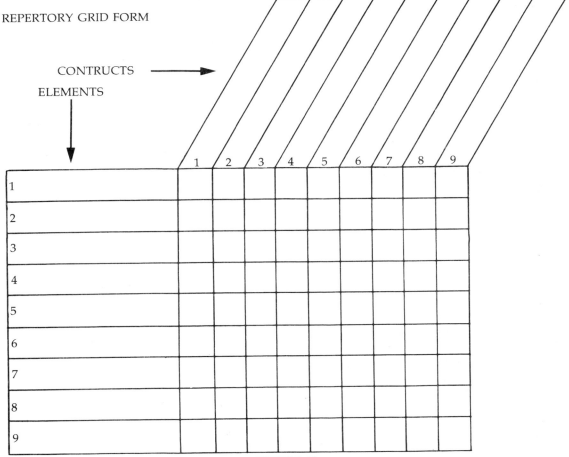

REPERTORY GRID FORM

FIGURE 19

doubt return to earlier chapters for more detailed explanation and try the simpler examples first.

STEP ONE: select elements 1, 2 and 3.

Ask yourself which two are more similar and which is the odd one out. Remember there is no correct answer – only your answer.

You might, for instance, select 1 and 3 as being similar in some way. Think over what it is that makes you feel they are similar. Try to get at important constructs that link the two elements together rather than such things as one and three being similar because they are connected with being in a factory and number two is concerned with being a playboy!

For example, a possible link might be: working only for money.

Now consider your opposite. In the example above this might be: doing what you like doing.

So the two poles of the first construct would be:

working for money ←→ doing what you like doing

Another person might link 1 and 2 together, with 3 being the odd one out. The connection might be:

outdoor work/meeting people, and the opposite:

office job/cut off from people.

Number 3 has been selected because you know that with the promised reorganization in your firm, your possibilities of meeting people will be limited. This change is one that you dread because you are a lively person who has a need to be with others.

It may be that you cannot see any change in work in the future, so you will need to write down the same answers for elements 1 and 3. In this case try to con-

sider how it is that these two differ from element 2.

Elements 1 and 3 may be working in a factory and element 2 be about running your own smallholding. Work out the difference in terms of constructs. You feel that the answer is:

being controlled ←→ freedom and independence.

Try not to be influenced by the examples given above. They are presented to provide you with an idea of the sort of constructs which might emerge. Yours are likely to be different. The whole purpose of the exercise is for you to get at the way you see *your* world.

Once you have elicited the two poles of your first contruct, you can either pause and consider its implications, how you feel about them and their possible connections with stress in your life; or you can complete the whole exercise and look at wider issues first. As most people find that the whole exercise usually takes them at least a few hours to complete you may feel that you should work on what you've already got and continue with other constructs later.

In many ways the whole point of the exercise is not to have a nice looking set of relationships, *but actually to work through the grid.* It is the insights that emerge directly or indirectly during the process that are of value to you.

If you decide to pause and consider the implications of the first construct, you can try the laddering exercise as you did when you examined more general questions of stress in your life in chapter three.

Ask yourself which pole of the construct you prefer. You remember that constructs are bi-polar, they consist of opposites:

love ←→ hate

soft ◄————► hard
interesting ◄——► boring

Some of the opposites may be unusual because they apply only to the person doing the grid, for example:

interesting work ◄——► depression

You can already see that someone with such a construct has difficulties if she or he does not get work that they consider interesting. Depression is the price paid.

Select your preference. Of the pair above, most of us would choose: 'interesting work'.

You might already see the beginnings of a dilemma. If the price you paid for not having interesting work was depression, how would you decide when the choice is between working for more money or doing a job you really like. To be rich and depressed or poor and enjoy yourself might be the outcome!

Whatever construct emerges for you, you do not at this stage make any major decisions like changing your job or starting a new career. You are only starting to explore meanings and possibilities. Later, you can consider a major change like what sort of work you would enjoy doing, could do and what money you need to live on. Even here the choice is not straightforward – it would depend upon the level of satisfaction compared with income. It could well be that doing work you'd like doing is not possible at the moment (you do not, for instance, have the necessary skills).

Let's continue laddering so that you can explore the importance of the meaning behind the pole of the construct you prefer.

With laddering you move up a structure of meanings, going from subordinate, less important meanings to more important superordinate ones. You create a hierarchy of constructs. Those constructs at the top of the ladder control or influence constructs lower down. It is more difficult to change superordinate constructs than subordinate ones.

Here is another example:

outdoors/meeting people ◄——► office/cut off from people

You might select as the preferred pole: outdoors/meeting people.

About your selection, you ask yourself why it is important to you to be the sort of person who prefers being outdoors meeting people. Your answer might be:

'It is important to me to be outdoors meeting people because I feel free and I find people stimulating.'

Two constructs have emerged here. One is 'feeling free' and the other 'finding people stimulating'. Both need to be laddered. If they were your constructs you would ask yourself why it is important to you to feel free.

Your answer might be:

'It is important to me to feel free because I feel I am really living, I feel I can breathe when I am in control of what I do'. Your opposite might be: 'being controlled'.

This may be as far as you can go with this part of the ladder because you have reached what is called a core construct.

You can see that an anticipated job in an office would not provide this sort of control and freedom – a possible cause of stress; certainly of dissatisfaction.

To complete our example, we need to look at the other superordinate construct which emerged. (In your laddering, it is quite likely that there is only one path to ladder).

The other part of the ladder might go something like this:

'I am the sort of person who likes to interact with people because this makes me feel alive'. The opposite might be: 'feeling dull, bored, not fully alive'.

Again there may not be much point in laddering this further as you are likely to come up with: 'this is what life is about for me'. This seems to be another core construct.

Two important core constructs have emerged: 'feeling alive' and 'feeling free by being in control'.

To recap: ask yourself which of the two poles of your first construct you prefer. Then ask why are you the sort of person who prefers that choice. A new construct will emerge. Decide on its opposite. Again select your preference and ask yourself why you are the sort of person who prefers this choice. Repeat the process until you feel you can go no further.

If you try helping someone else to do a grid, it is safer not to ladder with them. Core constructs can be very sensitive issues and need to be handled with care and considerable skill.

SECOND STEP: move on now to the next three elements. Select numbers 4, 5 and 6 and ask yourself which two go together. Write your answer and its opposite pole on the grid form.

In our example you might have selected 4 and 6 as similar with the two poles of a construct being:

place of friction ◄──► place of rest.

You can try out the laddering exercise about this as you did with the first three elements or you can complete the whole exercise first and look at it as a whole as well as in detail. In a way the method doesn't matter. Its aim is for you to elicit important constructs about your work life.

When you have pinpointed some important constructs connected with your work, you can start considering alternative meanings. There are many ways of perceiving the same set of events. Sometimes we are stuck because we can only see things one way. It is as if we are wearing blinkers and can only see directly ahead. Considering alternative meanings helps us develop innovative solutions to tackling problems.

For instance, your grid may suggest that 'control' is a key construct for you. Many studies have shown that when we feel that we are not in control we may become stressed.

One such study compared 'work pressure/no control' with 'work pressure/control'. Subjects in the 'work pressure/no control' group had enhanced cortisol levels. They felt uneasy and dissatisfied. These problems were absent in the other group. In another study a 'no-control' group also showed adverse symptoms such as poor sleep, psychosomatic illnesses and gastrointestinal disorders.

Not only 'control/pressure' can cause stress. Intellectually undemanding work without control also leads to similar problems. One research study reported increased adrenaline and catecholine for 'no control' groups although their work was undemanding compared with another group who were allowed discretion over how they carried out their work.

Stress started at work can continue at home. You remain irritable and fatigued. Leisure time does not aid recuperation. You stay unrested. You may not sleep well. The next day the process is repeated.

Examine your own work. Ask yourself how much control you have over what you do, how you do it and when you do it. Are you closely supervised? How does this compare with others in a similar job? Later we look at ways to help you deal with stress caused by lack of control. For some lack of control is not limited to work. It is more general. They feel controlled rather than in control.

REPERTORY GRID FORM

CONSTRUCTS ——▶

ELEMENTS

	YOUR PRESENT WORK	IDEAL WORK	LIKELY FUTURE WORK	HOME LIFE NOW	IDEAL HOME LIFE	LIKELY FUTURE HOME LIFE	SELF-DEVELOPMENT ACTIVITY NOW	IDEAL SELF-DEVELOPMENT ACTIVITY	LIKELY SELF-DEVELOPMENT ACTIVITY
	1	2	3	4	5	6	7	8	9
1 OVERLOADED – JUST ENOUGH CHALLENGE	1	3	2	1	5	4	1	3	3
2 TRAPPED – FREE	2	4	3	3	5	4	1	3	3
3 TOO FORCED – FLOWING	1	4	3	2	5	4	1	4	4
4 BEING PUSHED – TAKING IT EASY	2	3	3	2	5	4	1	3	3
5 UNEXPECTED – NOT SO	4	3	4	4	3	3	4	2	3
6 AS AT PRESENT – DIFFERENT	1	4	3	1	3	3	1	3	3
7 RESULTS ORIENTATED – SEEING WHAT RESULTS	1	3	2	3	3	3	1	4	3
8 LOTS OF EFFORT – MORE NATURAL	1	4	3	2	4	3	1	4	3
9 ORGANIZING – LETTING THINGS HAPPEN	2	3	3	3	4	3	1	5	3

FIGURE 20

Let's return to the repertory grid.

THIRD STEP: select elements 7, 8 and 9. Follow the same procedure.

NEXT STEP: continue with the selection order mentioned at the beginning of this section.

Place your constructs on the grid (figure 19).

What your grid provides is a starting point for you to consider alternative ways of seeing things, to develop new solutions and to change priorities. You can analyse further by allocating numbers to how the constructs fit each of the elements as you did in the earlier chapter.

If you feel that the first pole of construct number one fits with element number one give it the number 1. Place this in the box under the first element. If it only fits somewhat, allocate the number 2, if it is in the middle allocate 3; give 4 for a construct which does not completely fit and 5 for one which does not fit at all.

Follow the same procedure for the rest of your constructs. Then see which lines have similar ratings.

Figure 20 shows an example of a completed grid. See what you can work out from this grid. What is it likely to mean to the person concerned. What major problems might she have. What decisions might follow!

Consider the information from your grid along with your graph on the priorities you gave to the meta-themes connected with your work life. Look at the link between the two. Consider the implications of the constructs that have emerged, look also at the way they are linked together. Give a name for common clusters.

Next we move on to consider some of the conflict which arises from contrasting demands of home and work life.

TOPIC REFERENCES

Career Orientations:

Derr, C. Brooklyn, 'Career switching and organizational policies: the case of naval officer *in* Katz (ed.) *Career issues in human resource management*, Prentice Hall, 1982.

Derr, C. Brooklyn, *Career policies; theory and methods for career success*, Institute of Human Resource Management. Utah, 1982.

Derr, C. Brooklyn, *Managing the new careerist: the diverse career success orientations of today's workers*, Jossey-Bass, 1986.

Driver, J. J., 'Career concepts: a new approach to career research' *in* Katz (ed.) *Career issues in human resource management*, Prentice Hall 1982.

Instrumental and Privatized Worker:

Goldthorpe, J. H. and Lockwood D., *The affluent worker: political attitudes and behaviour*, Cambridge University Press, 1968.

Political issues:

Bottomore, T. B., *Class in modern society*, Allen and Unwin, 1965.

Kay, E., 'Middle Management' in

O'Toole, J. (ed.) *Work and the quality of life*, MIT Press, 1975.

Locked-in:

Quinn, R. P., 'Locked-in as a moderator of the relationship between job satisfaction and mental health' (unpublished). Research Centre, University of Michigan, 1975.

Type A and B behaviour:

Caplin, R.D. et al., 'Organizational stress and individual strain' unpublished PhD dissertation, University of Michigan, 1971.

Friedman, M. and Rosenman, R. H., *Type A behaviour and your heart*, Knopf, 1976.

Haynes, S. G. et al., 'The relationship of psychobiological factors to coronary heart disease in the Framlington study, *American Journal of Epidemiology* 111, 37. 1980.

Hunt, J., Managing people at work. McGraw-Hill, 1979.

Maslow, A., *The farther reaches of the human nature*, Penguin, 1971.

Existence and other needs continuum:

Alderfer, C. P., *Existence, relatedness and growth: human needs in an organizational setting*, The Free Press, 1972.

Life stages:

Erikson, Erik., *Childhood and society*, Paladin, 1978.

Control and Stress:

Frankenhauser, M. *et al.*, 'Psychobiological aspects of life stress *in* Levine, H. and Ursin, S. (ed.) *Coping and health*, Plenum, 1980.

Johansson, G. and Sanden, P.O., 'Mental load and job satisfaction of control operators'. *Rapporter No. 40*. Dept of Psychology, University of Stockholm.

CHAPTER 6

Work and home

Stress in your life can be caused by conflict between the demands of home and the pressures of work. As we have already discussed, it is not easy to find a balance between what is required of being a husband or wife, father or mother, son or daughter and making a successful career for yourself.

Priorities at work clash with what your children expect of you. You begin to feel guilty because you do not spend enough time with them but work pressures are so demanding that what you feel you need from a home is a place to recuperate and not to be faced with additional demands.

When your partner and children look to you to enliven their rather dull day; listen to their problems or share with them some of their excitement, you find you do not have the energy and – to be honest – the interest in being able to meet their needs.

As well as creating or adding to work-induced stress, home life can compensate and even remove some of the harmful effects of a day full of pressure. Kind, caring support from a partner or close friend reduces the effects of stress.

It is the quality of the relationship which matters – not the amount of time spent together. Stability of a good partnership or relationship with sympathetic friends or someone with whom you live, with its mutual reinforcement, wipes away the tensions of the day.

An unsatisfactory relationship which is hostile, critical and non-supportive not only fails to help you reduce stress – it increases it. The irritations created by working frictions, overload and general dissatisfaction carry over into the evening and these are added to by an unsatisfactory home life. Neither work nor home offers respite. You are trapped by both.

The relationship between work and home can take a number of forms. Evans and Bartolome suggest five possible relationships: spillover, independent, conflict, instrumental and compensatory. Let's look at three categories which cover most of these possibilities:

1 They can be INDEPENDENT of each other.
2 CONFLICT with each other or the tensions of one 'spillover' into the other.
3 Best of all your home life can COMPENSATE for work pressures or (more rarely) the other way around.

Your income fashions your standard of living and sets boundaries to what you and your family are able to do. It can provide holidays, private schooling for your children, it enables you to pursue hobbies, live in the sort of house that suits you, provides the possibility of private health insurance, enables you to contribute to your favourite charity and so on.

In addition to these obvious influences (which in themselves can reduce stress or at least compensate for it), work and home life may be quite separate or totally integrated with your work.

If it is independent, you depart in the morning, return in the evening and your work stays at work. That's where you mentally and physically leave it. Likewise you do not bring your home problems with you into your office. You can shut yourself off and concentrate on work or home, whichever is appropriate.

The two, however, may conflict. If both you and your partner work, the differing pressures of two careers and running a home lead to friction.

In some instances, both work in the same business and roles clash as the relationships of husband/wife or father/son etc get mixed up with business roles. It is difficult to separate the work roles of boss and secretary, manager and subordinate when you also have intimate personal relationships.

If you are career orientated, you accept the extra hours that your job dictates. You may expect your wife to act as an unpaid hostess for visiting business clients. When promoted you take it for granted that your family moves with you, sacrificing their friends and the local interests that they have carefully built up over the years. If they resist, you feel that they are being difficult. You view the world one way and they see it differently. No side is right. No side is wrong. Perceptions differ about the same situation.

Although still small in number but increasingly, in some families it is the female who has a career and the male who stays at home. Many relationships I know have broken up because the male could not accept the 'dominant' role of his partner.

'Spillover' is the way the effects of work intrude into home life. You leave work tired, driving through congested streets, battle against other road users getting more tense as you progress towards home. Once there, you find yourself too fatigued to be pleasant. Your needs, you feel, are for a drink and an evening slumped in an armchair, vaguely watching television. Your job pressures colour the quality of your home life.

Running a restaurant, a farm, small business, shop or workshop from or near your home makes it difficult to separate work from home life. Work penetrates your living space. Family members find it difficult to cut themselves off from work and so do you. But if worked through and the frictions discussed openly, this can be an enjoyable and fulfilling relationship.

A satisfactory combination is when home and work compensate each other. Your leisure activities balance out the demands of your job. If your work is hectic, your home becomes a place of peace. If your job bores you, you and your partner take up exciting hobbies. When your job needs only limited physical activity, you compensate by gardening, DIY, sports, rambling, swimming, climbing, jogging or cycling.

You need to consider how your work and home relationships contribute to stress. Here is an exercise which helps you do just that. As with some of the previous exercises, you can look at how you see things and then compare your perceptions with those of other members of your family.

This is how a completed chart might look (see figure 21).

You can see that the relationship need not be (and rarely is) only of one kind. It is usually a mixture. In this example, there is some compensation, some of the relationship is independent but there is also considerable conflict. In many cases, there is this sort of mixture.

HOME AND WORK STRESS RELATIONSHIP CHART

FULLY

PARTLY

VERY LITTLE

| | COMPENSATES | INDEPENDENT | CONFLICTS |

FIGURE 21

Next complete a similar chart about how you would like it to be:

Ask your partner to do the same exercise and examine how you differ:

As well as examining your differing perceptions of how you individually see things, you can explore ways in which conflict could be reduced. You start with bringing the conflict into the open. This may be that you see things differently but didn't realize it. There was a surface of commonality but an undercurrent of conflict. Or the friction may be open.

Another source of conflict is that you and your partner's ideal home/work relationship wishes differ. You can then explore what each wants, why it is so important to them and, from this, generate ways in which you both can get something of what you want. You can analyse exactly what it is that causes friction between you.

Move on then to finding why it is important for one person to have what they are asking for. For example, if you come home too tired to communicate with your partner, examine what this means.

The conversation might go something like this:

'Why is it so important to you that I talk

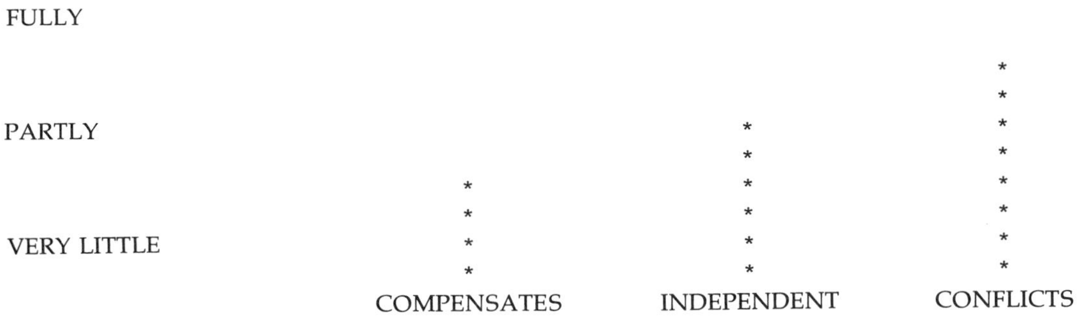

FULLY

| | | | * |
| | | | * |
PARTLY
		*	*
		*	*
	*	*	*
	*	*	*
VERY LITTLE
	*	*	*
	*	*	*

| | COMPENSATES | INDEPENDENT | CONFLICTS |

FIGURE 22

95

FULLY

PARTLY

VERY LITTLE

| | CONFLICT | INDEPENDENT | COMPENSATORY |

FIGURE 23

YOUR PARTNER'S IDEA OF WORK/HOME RELATIONSHIPS

FULLY

PARTLY

VERY LITTLE

| | CONFLICT | INDEPENDENT | COMPENSATORY |

FIGURE 24

to you when I come home?'

Reply: 'It is important because then I feel part of your life.'

'And this is important because. . . .'

Reply: 'I feel accepted by you and feel a real person not just an appendage to your life.'

You can see that one partner feels rejected, part of the furniture and not a full person. That's the meaning wrapped in talking to or being ignored by the partner.

Likewise the same exercise can be done with whoever comes home exhausted. It may end by feeling that this is the only

YOUR PARTNER'S IDEAL WORK/HOME RELATIONSHIP

FULLY

PARTLY

VERY LITTLE

| | CONFLICT | INDEPENDENT | COMPENSATORY |

FIGURE 25

way to survive.

Simple as it seems, this is a way towards real communication. It also frees the way towards developing creative solutions because you are dealing with real problems not just surface ones.

An additional helpful possibility is to learn to relax for half an hour each evening when you return from work, then have a shower to freshen up and perhaps do some exercises together.

You can also look exactly where the problems lie. If driving is a strain, you might consider public transport, or leaving later so that you miss the rush hour; or it may be that only particular days are difficult and you can examine what it is about these days that causes problems.

Work itself can be seen in many ways and our way of seeing it fashions the way we behave and how we live our lives. If you feel that a career is your main priority, your actions will reflect this. By considering alternative meanings, you give yourself choices. This might lead you to reduce the intensity of effort that you put into your career. Strangely, this could improve your working efficiency. It helps to be able to stand back and view things from a more detached perspective. It aids your judgement. It also reduces stress and this provides extra energy to tackle problems.

STRESS WITHIN THE JOB ITSELF . . .

The next major area to consider is the job itself. First we look at some general research findings about what has been established as stressful. You can then examine specific events within your own job which might cause you stress. This pinpointing of problem areas, helps you begin to take action directed to your exact needs.

The organization in which you work limits what action you are able to take. There is a range of organizational styles, from authoritarianism to participative. Your firm may be coercive and autocratic. You are told what to do and expected to get on with it. Control is tight and you are given little freedom to make your own decisions. The next step along this continuum is the paternalistic organization, where senior managers feel that they know what is in the best interests of employees. Next, there are firms which are consultative, they genuinely seek your views, consider them and sometimes use them; you feel that you have some stake in the company. A few firms are participative, where decision-making is fully shared.

The type of technology fashions to some extent a company's organizational style. In large batch or mass production technology, there is little room for shared decision making. In fact shop floor layout frequently makes ordinary interaction with fellow workers difficult.

Of course, the whole system could be changed as IBM did some years ago with their typewriter factory in Amsterdam and Volvo in their car plant, but these are exceptions. The cost of changing plant production methods is massive, so built into the job are tight systems and control. Things are becoming easier with the introduction of automation and robotics but at the price of fewer jobs. In process operations where only a relatively few skilled people are employed, there is much greater participation. This also applies in small batch or one-off products.

Things, however, are not that simple – most organizations are not monolithic. Various sections and departments within the company operate different styles. Some are heavily centralized and autocratic; others are more open.

Even within different sections, managers

adopt different styles. Some work through people, others make all the decisions themselves. Some pretend to consult their staff but in reality do not expect subordinates to have views of their own. Another approach is for a manager to appear tough but fail to follow things through. Others are inconsistent. Sometimes they seem open to your ideas, other times they tell you that you are not paid to think! You don't know where you are.

Other managers just aim to please, to be accepted as a friendly, warm-hearted, pleasant person by smoothing over potential friction. If you ask for a decision, they try to put off making one or attempt to guess what you want.

The situation is not just one-way. You respond to how you are told to work. If you have ideas and feel it is right that you should be consulted, you feel dissatisfied when your manager acts differently. Others of us just expect to be told what to do and get on with it. If your work orientation is to play safe, or you are only there for the money, you are more inclined to put up with things. This does not stop you feeling annoyed or stressed but you feel that's how things are.

There are considerable cultural differences. Some cultures *expect* to be consulted, others to be told what to do and these find that if they are called to a meeting to find out their views it is all a waste of time. One massive study carried out in forty countries showed that employees differed culturally in four areas:

1 Belief about power.
2 Uncertainty about economic and social life.
3 Working as a team or as an individual.
4 Androgyny.

When there is a belief that power should be shared and it is not, then there is dissatisfaction. Uncertainty about

economic life produces an inner drive to make life more certain – you work harder because you are pushed (by your inner needs) to do so. Where there is less of a feeling that life is like this, you need to be pushed externally to get the same results. Where you prefer to work as a team and cannot, or are forced to participate in meetings and your preference is to do your own thing, your job produces some strain, friction and stress.

Androgyny is the acceptance in a society of so-called traditional male and female qualities; for instance, 'male' qualities meaning being tough, results-orientated, power is the aim and big is beautiful; 'female' qualities being concern for people, nurturing, care and so on. If you feel one or the other is important and your company does not, then you feel out of tune with the company ethos.

There are dilemmas between the different orientations. If you feel life is uncertain, you are pushed to work but you may also feel that life is about being concerned with the needs of people and you cannot reconcile both.

Within each culture, there are also very considerable individual differences and notice that it is how you see things that matters. If you work on the assumption that your views are not wanted, you don't bother to offer them.

Perhaps some of your ideas were rejected in the past and now you feel that your contributions are not valued. But you may be wrong to generalize – it could be that once your specific idea was not acceptable or that you did not present it clearly enough, or that you did so at the wrong time.

You need to test out your beliefs to see if they are valid. There is generally room for some personal initiative. Many things are negotiable; but if you believe they are not, then you do not even try. Even in the poorest part of Belfast, some mothers were able to act with sufficient success to force the authorities to take action to improve family health services. In a concentration camp, Frankl, himself an inmate, ran a counselling service to help other prisoners to cope with their desperate plight.

Stress resulting from within your job is personal to you. Some of it, some of the time, will be common with what others find stressful.

To look more deeply at what stresses you and to help you pinpoint your specific problem areas, you can work through a repertory grid designed to establish the meanings behind those events you see as stressful.

As with the other exercises, you will have to work hard and think carefully. You now realize what has been emphasized many times, that there are no correct answers – only your answers.

The first stage is for you to select *elements*. These need to be actual work events that are specific but not general. Rather than, for example, selecting 'delegating', it is better to select something like: 'the time last week when I attempted to delegate and one of my subordinates refused to accept any additional tasks.'

Here is your list of elements to work through:

1 Select any work event in the last twelve months in which you felt stressed.

2 Select another work event which was tough or challenging in some way but which was not too stressful.

3 Select another work event which stressed you.

4 Select a work event in which you were quite busy but in which you felt you could cope.

5 Select a routine task which causes you some stress, irritation or frustration.

6 Choose a routine task which produces little or no stress.

7 A work task which you really like doing.

8 One which produces frustration.

9 Any significant event from your work last week (anything which comes into your mind – either satisfying, stressful or not – just what comes into your mind).

There are three others that you might like to add if you feel that they are appropriate:

10 Any important event or circumstance, in the last eighteen months, now over, but which still bothers you in some way.

11 Any anticipated event, certain or uncertain, which bothers you in some way.

12 Any non-work event which was stressful and which you feel intrudes into your working life.

Do not worry if you cannot select nine elements. Use whatever number you are able to think of. You can also choose more than the nine or twelve elements.

Write your elements (or an abbreviation of them) on the element row of the Work Construct Form (Repertory Grid).

Here are some examples of what others have written. Do not let them influence you, unless you really feel that they apply to you:

1 Preparing the departmental accounts when not all the information was available.

2 Looking at negative variances in the budget and holding a meeting of subordinates to cut costs.

3 Dealing with the boss when he refused to listen.

4 The time when travel arrangements went wrong and resulted in angry phone calls from delegates.

5 Searching through files for mislaid correspondence.

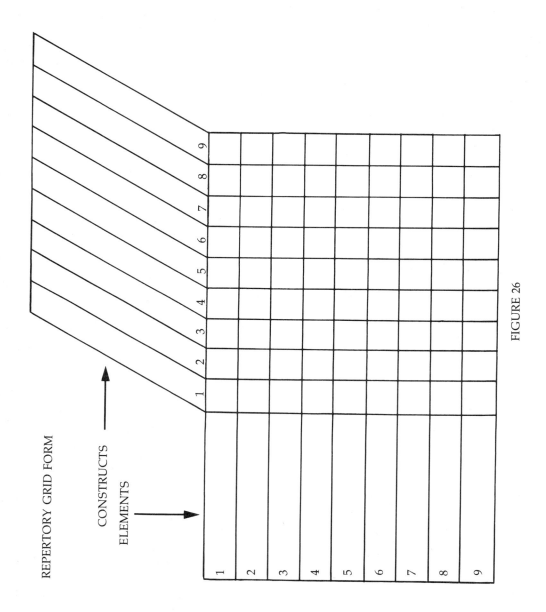

FIGURE 26

6 Using a word processor.

7 Chairing the 'creativity' meeting.

8 Chairing the meeting which spent hours amending the rules.

9 Dealing with a difficult but important question at a seminar.

10 Last year being 'moved sideways' (others saw it as demotion).

11 The rumours that the factory may be closed.

12 My mother's death.

Your list will be different – perhaps quite different, which is how it should be.

Now comes the difficult part. You'll need to think out what to write. The solutions may not come easily. It is not a test. All your answers are right for you. Often, it is the answer which first flashes into your mind which is the best one. You can always change it later.

First: select elements numbers 1, 2 and 3.

Ask yourself which two are more similar and which is the odd one out. You need to think deeply about the way these two are related. It is not sufficient to say that two were stressful and one was not, nor is it helpful to simply write down that two were done at the beginning of the week and the other always on a Friday.

You might for example say that two were 'time pressured', or two had the possibility of 'failure', or that the two paired elements gave you possibility of 'control' and the other did not, and so on.

Your answer is your first construct. This is a small way in which you see your work world. Constructs as you know by now are bi-polar, that is they have an opposite. You need to remember that you should select your opposite, not necessarily the one that you would find in a dictionary. For example, one manager gave 'depression' as his opposite to 'challenge', somebody else might have written 'boredom' or 'taking it easy'.

Write your first construct and its opposite in the first row of the Construct Form U.C.F. (Repertory Grid) or your copy of it.

Decide which is the 'positive', non-stressful construct. Write this on the right-hand side. This will help you to analyse your responses later.

Later, you can try more complex methods to examine results. Some will be suggested using a computer. (If you use a computer it doesn't matter which side you place the positive construct).

Here is an example of what you may have written:

possibility of failure ◄――――――► safe

or

time pressured ◄――――► no pressure

The important thing is for you to select your own constructs from the first three elements. If you are not happy with your initial choice, then certainly change your selection.

The next 'set' of elements you select is numbers 4, 5 and 6.

Again ask yourself which two are more similar, that is linked together in some way and which is the odd one out. Make sure you get a different construct from the first selection.

Think of what you feel is its opposite. For example, you may have thought that 4 and 6 went together because you were able to work speedily and that element 5 caused problems and frustrated you because you couldn't get results quickly enough.

Your constructs for this set might be:

work speedily ◄――――――► frustration

By now you should be gaining some skill in generating constructs and getting an insight into the way you see the world.

If you have some problems, try imagining some of the situations you have selected as elements. What feelings do they produce? Try letting your mind wander and then summarizing in one or two words how you felt. Then think of your opposite to that or those words. Frequently it is what comes immediately into your mind that is more meaningful. Sometimes you can start with the odd one out and then select your opposite of that.

Elements and the methods of selecting three at a time (called triads) is only a means to an end.

Your next selection is:

7, 8 and 9

Select the two which are more similar and think what construct links them. Work out your opposite and write both with the positive pole on the right hand side in the third row of the construct form.

Your first three rows of constructs may look something like this:

Time pressure/no time pressure
Failure possible/failure not likely
controlled/in control

You are now ready to go on with the next selection and build up a further picture of your individual world.

You do this by selecting the next set of numbers:

1, 4, and 7

Try to form a new construct out of these and not just repeat one that you used previously or a word which means the same.

Again write your selection down in the next row of the form.

You then continue with the following numbers:

2, 5 and 8
3, 6 and 9

1, 5 and 9
2, 3 and 4
6, 7 and 8

and if you have included further elements follow with these additional combinations:

10, 11 and 12
1, 2 and 10
5, 11 and 12

The best way to proceed is not to elicit all your constructs in one sitting. Do the first few and return later. You are quite likely to think of suitable constructs when you go about your daily work. Make a note of these and use them when you return to your repertory grid.

Remember also that you can always change your mind. If you think of more appropriate constructs or elements, do use them.

If you cannot think of different constructs for all the different combinations of elements, do not worry; you can work with a smaller number than nine constructs. If you think of more than nine (with the smaller list of elements, or more than twelve with the larger one), because you can see two or more ways in which two elements go together, include these as well.

What does it all mean? The completed list is your description of how you see your world as far as stress is concerned.

Here is a list that a client produced (using only seven constructs):

time pressure/no pressure
controlled/control
failure/success
depression/challenge
unclear objectives/objectives clear
too many bosses/one boss

Without going further we begin to get an insight into this client's (let's call him George) world. Stress seems to be connected with pressure, being controlled, having a task which might result in failure, not having clear objectives and reporting to too many bosses. Look at George's opposite of challenge. When there is no challenge to provide stimulation, excitement and fulfilment, George becomes depressed.

George pays a high price for work which does not challenge him. He also finds the thought of failure stressful. The difficult thing is that George (and the rest of us) cannot have challenge without the *possibility* of failure. Anything difficult we do might sometimes fail.

George has created a world in which it is impossible to live. Without challenge he is depressed. With challenge he risks failure. Either way George cannot win – at least within the way he construes this aspect of his work.

George also finds time pressure stressful but when we investigate more deeply we find that time pressure enhances the challenge that he likes in his job.

'Impossible task' might also be related to the likelihood of failure and so might unclear objectives.

George's world is becoming even more clear as we look at the way his constructs are related. We can see why he feels stressed.

Later on you will be able to examine your constructs in this way.

Constructs, as you have seen previously, can be linked so tightly that a problem in one area affects other areas to which it is related.

Constructs can also be totally independent of each other. Most people's construct system is a mixture, some constructs being closely related, others independent. As well as considering individual constructs, the structure of the way they relate is an additional tool in analysing your world.

But let's return to George. You've already seen that laddering is a way of developing the meaning of constructs.

Let's see how the technique works for George.

George was asked why it was important for him not to fail. He answered by saying that he needed others to see him as a success. He was then asked why it was important to him for others to see him as a success. George replied that underneath it all he felt a failure and didn't amount to much (he was in fact a successful manager). George said that he lacked a sense of worth and others seeing him as a success meant that they would not penetrate the front he presented to the world about being a success.

'They would not see into my worthlessness' said George.

'My greatest fear', continued George, 'is that the façade I present to the world might be smashed and they will see my worthlessness'.

Any chance of failure made George feel vulnerable. This was one source of his stress. Other aspects of George's personality sought challenge but within every challenge lurked the possibility of failure. George was in a trap.

Working through a repertory grid in this way helped George understand something of the nature of the trap he had set for himself. His next step was to realize that the trap was his own construction. Assessed against others, he was a successful manager.

George next looked at what advantages there were for him in maintaining the myth that underneath it all he was no good. At face value, there appears no benefit but as he maintained this part of his construct system, he must be getting something out of it.

To help work through this, George tried an 'ABC' analysis. Such an analysis helps to uncover hidden benefits for behaviour, cognition and feelings that are maintained despite their negative outcomes.

This is how it's done. You ask yourself what benefits there were for you in maintaining the negative aspects of a construct. This seems strange at first but once you start looking at things, advantages begin to emerge.

In George's case, being a failure meant that he did not have to accept fully his (perceived) overwhelming demands of the big real world. Digging deeper George felt that if he accepted full responsibility for what he did – the successes and the failures – he might not get the care and nurturing he needed. In George's world care and nurturing were reserved for the weak. This led George to talk about how, as a child, he got attention from his mother when she felt that he could no longer cope. When he looked vulnerable, his mother showered him with love. At other times (this was how George remembered it), his mother ignored him.

George also had an equally powerful message from his father: 'always meet challenges and aim for perfection'. The seeds of his present behaviour were set by his parents thirty years ago. Today George was still trying to fit an adult world into this outmoded childhood one.

Combined with George's insight came feelings of hopelessness, worthlessness and finally anger. Insights gained from doing a repertory grid often triggered off such associated memories and feelings. Releasing these helped George. He decided to move out of his trap. It wasn't easy, but knowing what it was all about helped.

George also began to look at his meaning of failure. Failing, for George, had validated his (hidden) view of himself. Further elaboration of this led him to reconstrue failure and look upon it as a positive, learning process. George also looked at the impossibility of always being perfect.

The important thing was that George was able to move in his life for the first time for many years. Such understanding helps reduce stress.

You can use the process George followed. Laddering consists of asking yourself why a particular construct is important to you. Your answer will contain a higher level and more abstract construct. Repeat the same question about this new construct and an even higher level one will emerge. Repeat the process and you will reach a stage where you can go no further and say something like: 'this is how it has to be', or 'this is what my life is about'. You have then reached a core construct.

Core constructs as you learned earlier are powerful. They 'govern' lower level subordinate ones linked to them. This is why you can experience considerable feeling about seemingly small events in your life. The event itself is minor but in your construct system it is linked to a powerful higher level construct.

You can also work through an ABC analysis. Look at negative constructs that are part of your life. Ask yourself what advantages you get out of them. Dig deep and you'll uncover benefits and begin to see why it is difficult to change.

When the benefits of so-called negative constructs are revealed, you can start considering other and more positive ways of getting what you want. There were more effective ways for George to get love and attention.

The next stage is to take a look at how constructs are linked to form part of a larger system.

Three methods will be explained. The first is straightforward and is similar to what you have already done. It will probably give you all the information you need. The other two are more complex

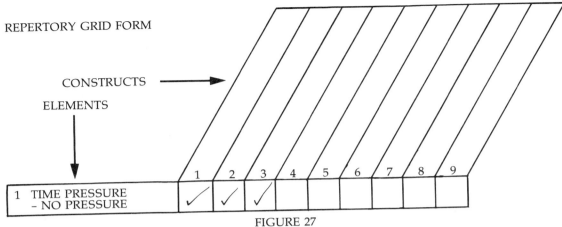

FIGURE 27

but they will give you a wider range of information.

Method 1

This is the method you followed previously. On the construct form for each row of bi-polar constructs tick all elements that link with the left-hand side of the particular construct. For example, if the first construct is:

time pressure ←——————→ no pressure,

then go along the row ticking all elements which seem to more or less link with it the left-hand side of the construct ('time pressure') as in figure 27:

If you feel that an element links with the right-hand side, 'no pressure', in our example, mark it with a cross. For example, element 4 links more with the right-hand side of the construct – 'no pressure' so the box underneath that element in the first row is ticked.

If neither side of a construct corresponds to an element mark it with an 'O'.

Your completed line will now look like figure 28:

You have analysed elements that are linked to the positive side of the construct, those that relate to the negative side and those in the middle which do not relate to either in particular.

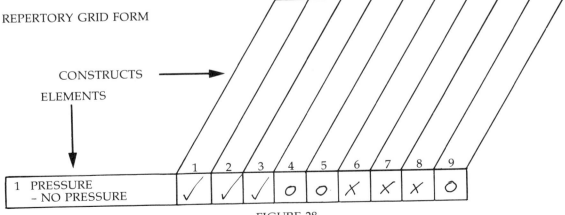

FIGURE 28

105

Now go to the second construct pair and follow the same procedure. Tick all constructs that link, cross those that do not and mark with an 'O' all those which do not apply or are in the middle.

At the end of the exercise you will have a mixture somewhat like the example above (except, of course, that your ticks, crosses and 'O's will be in different places).

Carry out the same procedure with all the other constructs until your form is complete with ticks where the left-hand side of the construct pole more or less fits an element, crosses where it does not fit and 'O' when either it does not apply or is in the middle.

Here is an example of a part of a completed repertory grid form (the names of the elements have been left out):

Each construct is a personal opinion. It is how a unique individual sees the situation with which he or she is faced. In the first construct: 'time pressure' ↔'no pressure', others may not feel any pressure at all in an identical situation.

Others may experience even more intense pressure because they lack the necessary skills or simply believe that they do. Some may create pressure as an excuse for failure, perhaps by making themselves so busy that they have no time to do the really important tasks – until they are forced to and then they can plead lack of time to do things properly.

Some of us need pressure because it is exciting. Working under a tight deadline gets the adrenaline going and we begin to feel alive. Type A personalities are like

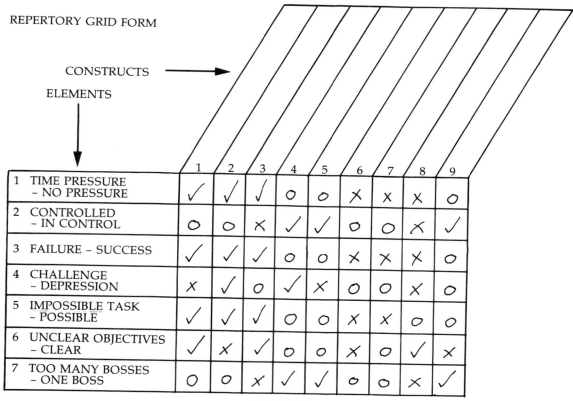

REPERTORY GRID FORM

CONSTRUCTS →

ELEMENTS

	1	2	3	4	5	6	7	8	9
1 TIME PRESSURE – NO PRESSURE	✓	✓	✓	O	O	✗	✗	✗	O
2 CONTROLLED – IN CONTROL	O	O	✗	✓	✓	O	O	✗	✓
3 FAILURE – SUCCESS	✓	✓	✓	O	O	✗	✗	✗	O
4 CHALLENGE – DEPRESSION	✗	✓	O	✓	✗	O	O	✗	O
5 IMPOSSIBLE TASK – POSSIBLE	✓	✓	✓	O	O	✗	✗	O	O
6 UNCLEAR OBJECTIVES – CLEAR	✓	✗	✓	O	O	✗	O	✓	✗
7 TOO MANY BOSSES – ONE BOSS	O	O	✗	✓	✓	O	O	✗	✓

FIGURE 29

106

this. They enjoy the feeling that they are battling against difficult odds.

Linking it together . . .

The final stage is to see how your constructs link together. You are seeking patterns, rather than single constructs.

The way you do this is to match up rows to see which are similar (say up to two differences in rows). You can do this visually by looking at your grid to see which lines have a similar pattern, or you can copy out the first row on another sheet of paper (make it exactly the same size as the original line). Move this copy down to the second line. Check whether it matches. Next go down to the third line and check. Repeat this by moving your copy of the first line down each line so that you can compare rows and see which are similar.

When you have compared the first line with all other lines, copy out the third row and compare it with the fourth, fifth and subsequent rows.

Repeat the process so that you are able to compare all lines with each other, ie compare line 3 with lines 4, 5, 6, 7 and 8, and then line 4 with lines 5, 6, 7, 8 and so on.

Repeat with line 5, comparing with lines 6, 7, 8 and 9, then line 6, comparing it with lines 7, 8, 9.

Continue until you reach the last but one row. Compare this with the final row.

In summary:

compare row 1 with rows 2, 3, 4, 5, 6, 7, 8 and 9
2 with rows 3, 4, 5, 6, 7, 8 and 9
3 with rows 4, 5, 6, 7, 8 and 9
4 with rows 5, 6, 7, 8 and 9
5 with rows 6, 7, 8 and 9

6 with rows 7, 8, and 9
7 with rows 8 and 9,
8 with row 9

In the last example in figure 29, you can see that rows 1, 3 and 5 are similar; 2 and 7 are similar whilst 4 and 6 do not link together with any other construct row.

This simple method – and especially your thinking about it provides insight into how stress patterns are built into your life.

An interesting point is that where a line is the exact, or nearly an exact, opposite to another line then there is what is called a negative correlation. If you reverse your construct poles, you can then form another link.

The last stage is to make it easy for yourself by drawing the relationships. Simply draw lines showing how contructs are linked together.

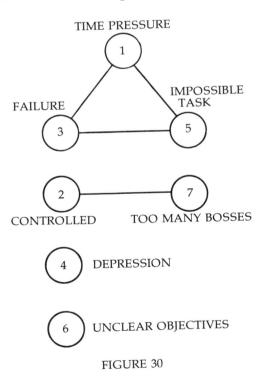

FIGURE 30

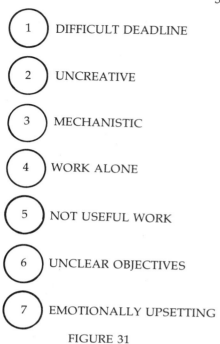

1. DIFFICULT DEADLINE
2. UNCREATIVE
3. MECHANISTIC
4. WORK ALONE
5. NOT USEFUL WORK
6. UNCLEAR OBJECTIVES
7. EMOTIONALLY UPSETTING

FIGURE 31

The first example is taken from the previous grid. It shows a pattern of constructs in which there are four separate parts. 1, 3 and 5 are linked; 2 and 7 are linked; 4 is alone and so is 6.

The next example in figure 31 shows a system in which there are no real links.

The last example in figure 32 shows a construct system in which everything is attached to everything else.

When you draw your own patterns, you may find that all your constructs are linked, presenting you with a tightly integrated system. Think of the practical implications of this in your daily life. It may mean that if one construct is affected, so are the others. Look at the negative end of the poles of each construct. This could be the price you pay for failure in one part.

Your system might be more similar to the second example, each individual con-

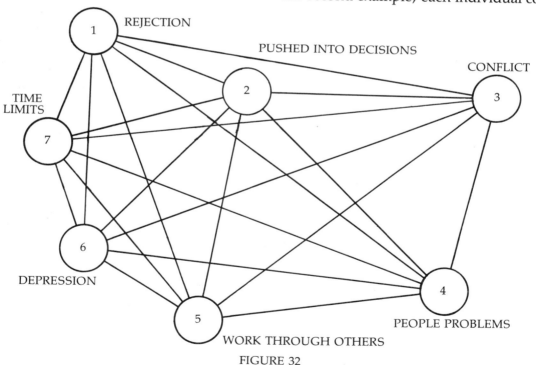

FIGURE 32

108

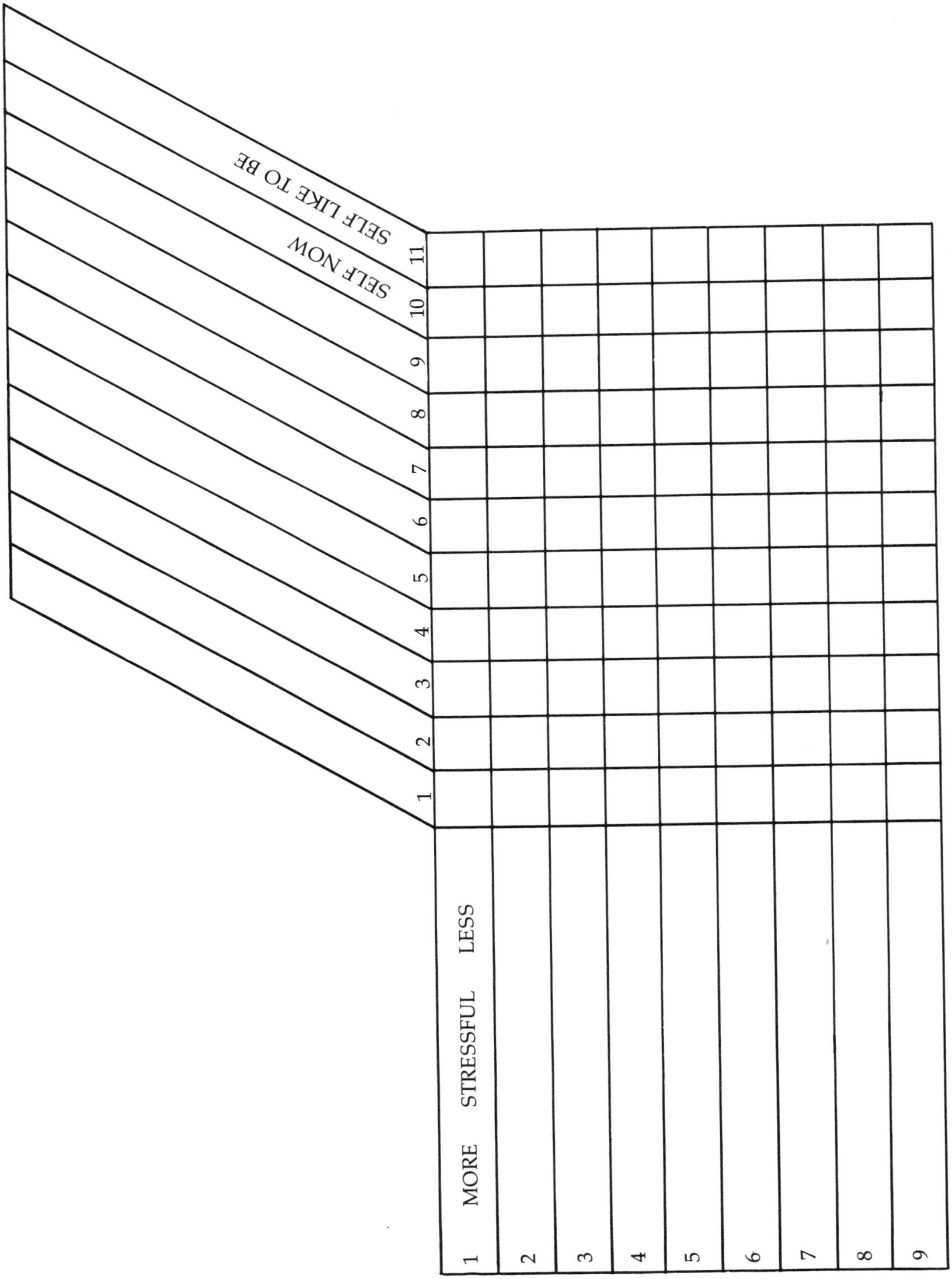

FIGURE 33

111

Two additional elements have also been included in columns 10 and 11:

self now
self-like-to-be

You may remember you did something like this in a previous exercise.

Mark every element which corresponds with 'more stress' with a tick, those which do not with a cross and those in the middle with an 'O'.

You can now see which work events (your original elements) are stressful and those which are not. This will of course correspond to your original selection of events to fit the element descriptions but you may grade some of them in the middle rather than being so stressful. You can also take a look at how 'self now' fits in with your overall stress grading. Did you place a tick, cross or zero against it? How does it differ from 'self-like-to-be'? This is an indication of how near you are (as far as stress is concerned) to the person you'd like to be. In the next section you can use a more refined grading system and measure the difference between the two selves.

Also see how you've graded the two selves as far as the other constructs are concerned. This gives you a further idea of how close you are to the person you'd like to be.

List the constructs where you'd like to change. Write out a description of yourself now using the construct gradings. Use the third person, that is talk about yourself using 'you', not 'I'.

For example (taken from one of the earlier grids):

'Mary sees herself as under considerable time pressure. She does not ask to be someone who has no pressure. In fact she likes it at times but what she has at the moment is too much for her.'

'Mary also feels as if she has no control over her life. She seems to be pushed by work pressures and this is similar to her home life. It is as if she has to respond to demands made on her.'

'She sees herself not as a failure but as one who has yet to make the grade. In fact she is afraid of failing despite the fact that she demands challenge in her work. She can see a conflict here with her need for less pressure.'

'What really upset Mary is to feel that what she is given to do is really impossible. Her boss frequently says: 'If you don't try, you won't know whether it is possible or not'.

'Mary likes to know where she is and what is expected of her. In her present set up at work, she does not really know what her objectives are. Her boss seems reluctant to spell them out. In fact they both seem to avoid discussing the issue. I wonder why she wants to be clear but doesn't do too much about it. Mary's other main problem as far as work is concerned is that she works for too many bosses, yes – she does officially report to one boss but members of the management committee all seem to think they can call on her to help them. Come to think of it, she always says 'yes' to their requests – no wonder they keep on asking.'

'Mary as she would like to be seems a long way from where Mary sees herself at the moment. The things that she really needs to tackle are.....'

All this description was taken from information from the earlier grid. As you do your own, add any bits that you think are appropriate.

Put it away for a few days and then reread it. You might be surprised! One client working through this exercise realized that her whole problem centred around the clash between her successful work role and the pressures on her to get married, have children and 'settle down'. In some ways she wanted to but also valued her independence which she was sure would be threatened if she married. Knowing what it was all about was, in itself, a relief. She could see her dilemma clearly and was able to set priorities and face up to what she was sacrificing by making them. She did move forward in her life, realizing that nearly every major choice means accepting some loss.

TOPIC REFERENCES

Work and home conflict:

Kanter, A.D., *Work and family in the US*, Sage, 1977.

Willensky, H.L., 'Work, Careers and Social Integration, in *International social science journal*, 12.243.60. 1960

Evans, P.A.L. and Bartolome, P.A.L., *The relationship between professional life and private life*. (Unpublished.)

CHAPTER 7

A look in more detail

A more refined way of analysing your grid is to quantify how much each construct links to each element.

Instead of using ticks, zeros and crosses, you use numbers; either 1–5 or 1–7. This is how it works: if the left-hand construct fits exactly with an element, you allocate the number 1; if it fits to some extent, allocate 2; if it doesn't apply or is in the middle, allocate 3; you allocate the number 4, if it is somewhat opposite to the left-hand construct. Lastly place a 5 if the left-hand pole of the construct does not fit the element at all; it is completely opposite. With a range of 1–7, you can show even finer differences.

Thus if you feel that 'time pressure' fits exactly with preparing departmental accounts, you allocate point 1. If it doesn't fit at all you allocate point 5.

Here is an example of a grid based on 1–5 points (leaving out the labels for the elements) (see figure 34).

You analyse the results in the same way as you did on the previous exercise with ticks, 'O's and crosses. It it more difficult to do visually but as some people seem to be able to do it easily, try it yourself.

If you find it a problem to see the relationships visually, copy out the first line on another sheet of paper, making the divisions the same size as the original. You can then place this first line against the second line and compare how similar they are. Move on to the third line and so on with all other lines. Then do the same

with the second line, comparing it with lines 3 to 9; then continue with line 4, comparing it with lines 5 to 9 and so on. Summarizing:

Start by comparing line 1 with lines 2, 3, 4, 5, 6, 7, 8 and 9

then compare line 2 with lines 3, 4, 5, 6, 7, 8 and 9

then compare line 3 with lines 4, 5, 6, 7, 8 and 9

then compare line 4 with lines 5, 6, 7, 8 and 9

then compare line 5 with lines 6, 7, 8 and 9

then compare line 6 with lines 7, 8 and 9

finally compare line 8 with line 9.

You are looking for lines which resemble each other. If there are just one or two differences in each line, you can say that the lines are closely related.

If you look at the last example shown above, you can see two clusters where the lines are similar. These are lines 1, 3, 4 and 5 for one cluster; lines 7 and 9 form the second cluster.

It looks as if 'time pressure', 'failure', 'depression' and 'being given a (perceived) impossible task' are connected in some way. It could be that 'impossible' tasks are those which have insufficient time available to carry them out and are likely to lead to failure. The payoff for failure in this example might be depression.

REPERTORY GRID FORM

CONSTRUCTS ⟶

ELEMENTS ↓

	1	2	3	4	5	6	7	8	9
1 TIME PRESSURE – NO PRESSURE	1	3	5	1	3	2	4	5	5
2 CONTROLLED – IN CONTROL	3	4	5	5	5	2	4	3	3
3 FAILURE – SUCCESS	1	3	4	1	3	2	3	5	5
4 CHALLENGE – DEPRESSION	1	2	5	1	3	1	4	5	5
5 IMPOSSIBLE TASK – POSSIBLE	1	1	5	1	3	1	4	5	5
6 UNCLEAR OBJECTIVES – CLEAR	2	3	3	5	3	1	1	4	1
7 TOO MANY BOSSES – ONE BOSS	4	3	1	1	1	2	3	4	1
8 INTERESTING – BORING	1	2	3	5	4	2	5	2	1
9 RESPONSIBILITY – NONE	4	3	1	2	2	3	3	4	1

FIGURE 34

The other cluster suggests that too many bosses is somehow related to responsibility.

If you find clusters in your grid – and you are quite likely to – you need to think out the implication of what they mean to you. Give each a name which represents the constructs it covers.

This might be a different name or a name taken from one of the constructs which you feel is more important in that cluster. In the example discussed, we might allocate 'possible failure' to the cluster. You have to ask yourself whether the name you give 'feels right' for you.

You then work on the clusters. It is here that stress patterns emerge. Ask yourself what is the opposite to the name you've given to your clusters. The opposite may or may not be an opposite from one of the individual constructs within the cluster.

In our example, we might feel that 'appearing successful' is right. Thus we have a new construct:

possible failure ⟷ appearing successful

You can then ladder and elaborate the construct. The negative side seems interesting. It appears that it is not success or failure that matters but not being seen to fail. Stress might arise when we are

115

likely to be found out for our failures and if we can get away with it we feel OK. You could then look at how much energy is used to avoid being caught out. Later you may find that you are able to face failure because you have redefined it in some way.

You can see the power of this approach. Stress will be reduced because failure becomes a learning exercise as we suggested earlier and energy is not needed to avoid others seeing our mistakes. We don't have to pretend we are perfect and use our mental resources, making sure others see us this way – and no longer feel stressed because we may be caught out.

This type of analysis provides an insight into your mental world. It is like a photograph. It enables you to capture some representation of how you see things. Often these are ways of seeing things which were not fully realized before. Like a photograph, you recognize yourself, but as you are an observer you are able to consider yourself as an outsider would. It is the start of an exploration.

Of course, this emergent construct structure is only a small part of your mental world. It is limited, incomplete and simplified. Nevertheless, it does help pinpoint your stressors. You can then channel your energies into more appropriate areas and not deal with generalities.

Let's see how it works with another example. You saw previously how one manager could not delegate because he found losing control too threatening. His initial problem was work overload. To attempt to reduce his overload by getting him to delegate, providing additional staff, increasing his management skills by sending him on training courses would have been to miss the main cause of his problem.

His problem needed to be tackled at its root. Learning to relax would have reduced some adverse effects of his stress but the main point would have been ignored. Using grids and similar tools helps ensure that you do not miss the main points of your stress problems.

As with the previous simplified grids, you need also to look at lines which are exactly or almost exactly opposite to other lines. These also form a cluster because the right-hand side of a bi-polar construct links with left-hand sides of other constructs.

Statistically, there is a negative correlation. Data can relate to other data in three ways:

positively
negatively, or
not at all

Within the first two, there are shades of how well they fit together. A complete fit is $+1.0$, a partial fit $+.5$, a small fit, is say, $+.2$ (with, of course, all the other figures in between). A negative correlation has the same principle, except that it is represented by the minus sign $(-)$: -1.0 is a complete opposite and so on. Zero (0) is the figure given to no relationship at all.

Correlations do what you were doing, when you decided that lines linked together, but with greater precision.

You do not need to understand statistics to get value out of your grid analysis. As has been emphasized previously, it is the process of working through them that is the major value.

Forgetting about statistical negative correlations, you can see from the example below that lines 1 and 2 present opposites. In the first column of element 1, 5 is opposite 1; in column 2 etc.

What does this mean? In this example, for some personal reason, 'mechanistic work' presents a 'clear' way of working. 'People related' (meaning relationship with people) however, is ambiguous.

REPERTORY GRID FORM

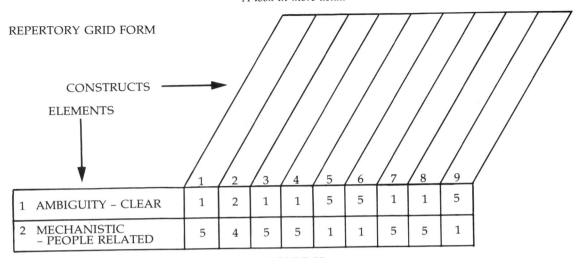

CONSTRUCTS

ELEMENTS

		1	2	3	4	5	6	7	8	9
1	AMBIGUITY – CLEAR	1	2	1	1	5	5	1	1	5
2	MECHANISTIC – PEOPLE RELATED	5	4	5	5	1	1	5	5	1

FIGURE 35

Dealing with tasks such as arranging production schedules is straightforward. You 'clearly' know what to do. It is people who are uncertain. They cannot be organized as if they were machines and their output placed in a production chart and left at that. At times they are irrational and unpredictable. This may be the source of stress for the originator of the grid shown above.

Remember the special definition of 'hostility'. We defined it as: 'trying to force the world into the way we see things although we are aware (at some level of consciousness) that our definition is not valid'.

Hostility might apply in our example. Acting as if people are predictable at all times results in being let down. If you continue to plan on this assumption, having been let down in the past, you are going to have problems. There is a mishmash between reality and the way you see things. You become angry when people let you down by not fitting in with your predictions of them. It doesn't help with relationships. It doesn't get the job done effectively. Perhaps we are coming to the heart of the stress problem in this small example.

Many of us know people who live their lives as if the world was different from what it is.

If you have done the extended grid with the 'more stressful ◄─► less stressful' construct and the additional 'self now' and 'self-like-to-be' and you grade each box with a scale of 1, 2, 3, 4 or 5, you can measure much more precisely how near you are to who you want to be. Unfortunately, you cannot just consider the differences because they may cancel each other out.

At a basic level just go through each, noting how near each is to what you want. Better still, do a correlation. If you don't know how, try following the instructions on a calculator or get a friend to do it for you.

If the correlation between the different selves is a negative one, that means that you are far from being the sort of person you'd like to be. If it turns out to be, say, +.5, then you are somewhere near your goal but you have quite a way to go. If you are as you wish to be, then you must feel satisfied or your life lacks any real goal or challenge.

A STEP INTO STATISTICS . . .

Skip this chapter if statistics turn you off. However, you might be surprised at how easily you could get to grips with some of the ideas outlined.

Instead of visually seeing how the figures relate to each other, you can do a correlation analysis (use Spearman's rank correlation coefficient as the data is ordinal).

This analysis provides a correlation matrix. It shows statistically how each figure in your grid relates to every other figure, either positively or negatively. Remember the negative and positive relationships? The matrix indicates intensity of relationships as well as their degree of significance. The degree of significance is the likelihood of whether the results are just chance only.

There are computer programs which will analyse these correlations into clusters (remember that's what you have been doing), or into principal components or common factors (factor analysis). These last two are different ways of seeing underlying relationships. Each type of analysis has advantages and some disadvantages. A principal component analysis does use your own words for the construct to which other constructs are linked. A factor analysis provides new underlying constructs to which others are linked. In practice, if you put the same data through different statistical programs, the results are usually similar.

Do not worry if you do not have access to a computer or statistics frighten you. Your previous analyses provide you with sufficient insight to help you pinpoint the stressors in your life. If you are interested in more details about the statistical analyses of grids, there are one or two good books on the subject. They are mentioned in the recommended reading list at the end of this book.

A further extension is to consider how resistant to change are your various constructs. You can do what is called a 'resistant to change' grid. Details of this and other grids can be found in the recommended books. There are also courses which help you become proficient in analysing grids if you are interested in going further in this direction. But remember that grids and all the other techniques are only a means to an end.

A REMINDER . . .

Let's pause for a moment and remind ourselves where we are by returning to our original framework for stress:

1 A trigger event, situation or set of circumstances which may be chronic or acute; in the past, happening now or anticipated; real or imagined.

2 The perception given to that event in which we see some form of threat with which we feel unable to cope. It is (we believe) beyond our resources.

3 The physiological arousal resulting from our perception.

4 The behaviour that follows our arousal, which may itself feed into the system as we notice our inability to cope with the original stressor.

We mentioned earlier that sometimes stress starts with the third item. A chemical imbalance resulting from some food to which we are allergic creates conditions similar to stress. We then seek conditions in the environment to fit in with our mood. In fact we 'construct' what we need out of environmental possibilities.

Often is is the way we view the external trigger which sets off our stress reaction. The system is also interactive. Our behaviour is one of fight/flight/freeze. We note how we react and then have that fact to deal with. We worry about being worried, become anxious about being anxious and are afraid of our fear. In some instances it is this 'chain reaction' which is the major problem. For example, in giving a presentation to a group it is usual to become aroused, to feel the increase of adrenaline, to be more alert and to perspire. If we start to worry about what's happening to us, we add to our stress.

Sometimes we deny that we are stressed. At some level of awareness, we know that a situation is threatening to us. It is too much to face so we deny it. We act as if it was not there. Situations do not go away. Trying to force the world into our framework, despite evidence to the contrary, means that the pressures on us remain. We do not attempt to solve the problem, only ignore it. We may get away with it but usually, sooner or later, it gets worse and we are forced to act.

We may intellectualize, that is distance ourselves from the problem. We feel it does not affect us personally, it is out there, not really part of us. It is as if we have a balance sheet showing we are bankrupt and all we do is to examine it as an interesting statement of how to lay out the assets and liabilities of a company.

Another strategy is to project our problem or faults on others. It is all *their* fault. They never produce good work, they always let us down, they don't consider others etc. What we are doing is making sure that we hide from ourselves what we already know! We don't tackle the problem, because we dare not face the frightening consequences that it holds for us.

These activities get us nowhere. We have a lot of energy locked up in the problem. The pity of it is that if we were to face what we need to face, we are likely to find it different from what we think it is – usually more manageable. We are hiding

from an imagined aggressor. The aggressor is powerful – but only because we give it power. The answer does not lie in pretending we are not threatened nor in learning better ways to fight or run away but by looking at what it is that we think threatens us. We have more power than we think.

There are many levels at which the stressful situation can be examined.

1 Our perception of the situation may be open to different and more constructive interpretations. Ask yourself why it is that some people do not find similar situations so stressful.

2 Even if our perceptions match an external reality, our interpretation of what should be done can be examined and alternative actions considered.

3 If our behaviour cannot be modified, we can examine the way we construe our actions. Our stress might be connected with feeling that we are failures. Stress results, partly at least, from the way we see ourselves. We do the right thing in the right way, but never feel that our efforts are good enough. We may, in fact, achieve our main objective but note only the small failings in our activities.

4 We may know what we need to do. We may lack the necessary skills but could set about acquiring them. We could learn to delegate more effectively, write better reports, improve our presentation skills, become proficient with a computer and so on. We need not be stuck at our existing level of proficiency.

Later on in this book, ways will be suggested in which you can increase your proficiency.

5 We can create a social support group with whom we can share our problems.

6 We can start taking care of ourselves, learning to pace our work, building in suitable breaks, taking up exercise, we can improve our diet, cut our smoking, reduce alcohol consumption, we can

make sure that we have compensating leisure activities. We can learn to relax, both during the stress situation and generally, so that harmful physical effects are minimized.

If we are living in overload, almost any one of these items will reduce our stress to a more manageable level. But why stop here, when we could take it further and begin to feel on top of life.

By relaxing each day you will find yourself becoming more peaceful and at ease. This in turn makes your problems seem less severe, leading to a freeing of your energies.

To see how it all works, we are going to look at a number of case studies. These are all real people. They were all managers from the same company in The Netherlands, aged between thirty-five and fifty-five years and roughly at the same level in their firm. You will see that there are many causes of stress, some commonalities (although below the surface these may differ), and the way constructs link together differs considerably.

Case No 1: Henk

This is how a principal component computer analysis showed the relationship (correlation) between Henk's constructs:

Constructs

	1	2	3	4	5	6
1		−.98	−.98	−1.0	−1.0	−.78
2			.95	.98	.98	.75
3				.98	.98	.89
4					1.0	.78
5						.78

Each of these correlations showed the strength of the connections between constructs. You may remember that 1.0 is a

REPERTORY GRID FORM

HENK	1	2	3	4	5	6
1 REST – ACTIVE	1	4	1	5	3	4
2 CREATIVE – BEING LED	5	2	5	1	4	2
3 DEFINING – WAITING AROUND	5	3	5	1	3	2
4 CHALLENGE – ROUTINE	5	2	5	1	3	2
5 PROBLEM SOLVING – LACK OF ACTION	5	2	5	1	3	2
6 ORGANIZING – BEING MANIPULATED	5	5	5	1	3	1

FIGURE 36

HENK'S STRESS CHART

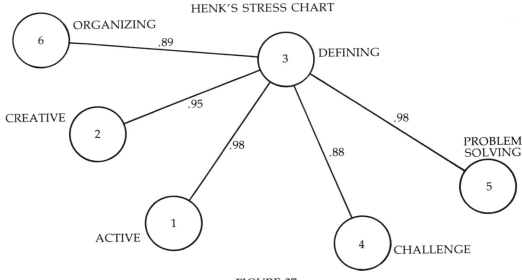

FIGURE 37

complete fit. You use the table by looking at the first row to see how construct number 1 relates to constructs 2, 3, 4, 5 and 6. You look in the second row to see the relationship between constructs 2 and 3, 4, 5 and 6. In the third row you have construct number 3 with its relationships with constructs number 4, 5 and 6 and so on.

(For those who are interested, the relationships are two-tailed and all were significant $p < .05$ or $< .01$ except for construct number 2 with construct number 6.)

If you draw Henk's stress chart, you can see how everything related to everything else (see figure 37).

Henk's main construct (principal component) was number 3 'Defining'. By this Henk meant knowing what he needed to do and being able to get on with it. To Henk this also meant being active, creative, having challenging work, solving problems and getting organized. What stressed Henk were the negative poles of these constructs: waiting around,

resting, being led, having only routine work, lack of action and being manipulated.

Henk's stress was all connected with not getting things done which he liked doing. He then began to look at the elements that he had supplied which enabled him to elicit his constructs. These gave further clues to where his problems were. They were connected with the reorganization of his department and, to a lesser extent, his need to report on the activities of his department. This latter part was not too difficult to deal with. Henk needed to develop better report-writing skills.

The other problem was larger. It meant discussing the reorganization with his manager and seeing what could be changed. Henk was set the task of getting some of the changes he needed. This was to be his challenge, action plan and problem solving exercise. You can see that Henk's way of setting about his stress problem was, in itself, the way of working that he favoured. He turned his problem into a challenge – and he liked challenge!

He also started a relaxation programme of twenty minutes twice a day.

The next case from the same group of managers was the exact opposite in the way constructs were structured.

Case No. 2: Jan

Jan's constructs were not linked at all. You can see this from the very small correlation between constructs:

Constructs

	1	2	3	4	5	6
1		$-.54$	$-.55$	.39	$-.33$	.41
2			$-.2$	.11	.09	.11
3				$-.64$	.56	$-.3$
4					$-.54$	.11
5						$-.53$

No correlation was linked to any other at the p.05 or .01 levels. This means that the (small) relationships which did exist were likely to be there by chance only.

Jan's grid looked like this (see figure 38).

Everything was separate. This meant that Jan, unlike Henk, had to fight his stress on many fronts.

You can see this more clearly from the graphic representation of Jan's grid (see figure 39).

It looked as if Jan had a general stress problem related to most of his work. If things didn't go well, he felt frustrated. he then tried harder, which resulted in further frustration if things didn't turn out the way he wanted. He also liked to see some end results. If he was part of a large chain, he would never really know how his contribution turned out, adding to his stress. Other work left him physically exhausted because of the quantity needed to be produced in the time available.

REPERTORY GRID FORM

CONSTRUCTS ⟶

ELEMENTS

JAN

	PREPARATION WORK	CLIENT VISIT	DIFFICULTIES WITH SUBORDINATE	USING NEW PROGRAM	NEW WORD PROCESSOR	DIFFICULT JOURNEY
	1	2	3	4	5	6
1 FRUSTRATION – EASY FLOW	1	3	2	3	1	2
2 GETTING END RESULTS – NO REAL RESULTS	2	1	4	2	5	1
3 PHYSICAL EXHAUSTION – EXHILARATION	4	3	2	2	4	5
4 MECHANISTIC – INTERACTIVE	2	5	5	2	2	1
5 POSITIVE CONTRIBUTION – NEGATIVE	2	1	3	2	3	5
6 OVER POWERED – IN CONTROL	2	4	2	4	4	2

FIGURE 38

1 FRUSTRATION

2 NOT GETTING END RESULTS

3 PHYSICAL EXHAUSTION

4 MECHANISTIC

5 NEGATIVE CONTRIBUTION

6 OVER POWERED

FIGURE 39

Examining the elements listed by Jan showed which tasks caused problems. We see that he graded 2 both dealing with a difficult subordinate and using the new computer program. Both of these can be considered in more depth. It may be that dealing with a difficult subordinate was a 'one-off' occasion, or perhaps Jan found it tricky to deal with difficult members of his staff.

A 'one off' problem, which is over, need not be bothered with, other than by talking it over and releasing any unexpressed emotions still locked up from the encounter. Jan thought back to see if he could recall any similar occasion. There were many. It was not just a 'one-off', over-and-done-with stressor. Jan then probed deeper to see what it was about these incidents which bothered him.

Jan's investigation led him to see that he found it difficult to handle aggression – either his or other people's. He role-played the encounter and then repeated it, trying different approaches. He found that he tended to hold back initially from expressing any disapproval and then moved from this passive approach into

becoming too aggressive. He began to look at the difference between assertion and aggression and to practise some of the techniques. Jan learned something about himself from recalling episodes related to one of his constructs. He was going to follow this up by taking a course in becoming more assertive.

His other task was to find out what it was that made him so exhausted after certain activities. When he looked at this, it turned out to be 'unfinished work'. He worked quite well until he realized he would not complete what he set out to do (his objectives were unrealistic). As soon as he saw a mass of unfinished tasks, he felt drained of energy.

Through laddering, Jan looked at why it was important for him to have tasks completed and out of the way. His answer was that he then felt free. He followed this further and saw that being free meant that he could do what he wanted to do. If he was reminded of unfinished tasks, he tended to brood over them and this spilled into his leisure time. They spoilt his evening and sometimes his weekend as well. He could not enjoy himself when he thought of all the work waiting for him to complete.

He set to work on working out a 'production control' system for his work. This was a simple schedule which would tell him in advance what needed to be done and when. He then revised it so that it became realistic.

As an exercise, Jan deliberately left some tasks unfinished and went out to enjoy himself.

Jan had difficulties in handling work that did not flow well. He examined these. The main problem was interruptions. He looked further and found that he actually encouraged them. He found it difficult to say 'no'. He also found it difficult to switch from one subject to another as the need arose.

Jan also listed the main frustrations in his job and placed them into various categories. From this information, he did a Pareto analysis. A Pareto analysis shows how 80 per cent of main categories are caused by about 20 per cent of possible reasons. Deal with the 20 per cent and you remove 80 per cent of the problems. You limit your efforts and get large rewards. The effort in tackling the rest may not be worth the trouble.

As stress was connected with many different parts of Jan's work life, it was important for him to learn to relax generally and acquire the skill of being able to relax in potentially stress-inducing situations.

Jan also needed to learn to pace his work and take breaks. Some of us can manage only half an hour without a pause, others can go on for three hours or so. Individuals differ considerably in their capacity for sustained work. You need to find your own level. Beware of modelling yourself on others. You may be expending more effort despite less time before a break than someone who continues for twice as long. The break need only be five minutes or so. Get up, move around perhaps have a coffee and if possible a change of scene.

In a similar manner, Jan looked through the other parts of his grid and worked out his own individual stress reduction programme. Unlike Henk he had to work in a large number of areas.

Here is another grid, again with different problems. It shows how some constructs are linked into larger clusters and others are separate.

REPERTORY GRID FORM

CONSTRUCTS →

ELEMENTS

TREES

	NEW SCHEME	REVISED PROCEDURES	TRAINING NEW SUBORDINATE	SYSTEM Z INTRODUCTION	STARTING TEAM WORKING	EXTERNAL LIAISON	NEW WORK SCHEDULES
	1	2	3	4	5	6	7
1 FAIL – SUCCEED	5	1	1	3	3	4	2
2 EASY – DIFFICULT	1	4	3	4	3	5	4
3 RESULTS SLOW – IMMEDIATE	1	1	1	3	1	2	1
4 GOOD QUALITY – POOR	1	5	5	3	4	4	4
5 HAVE KNOWLEDGE – LACK KNOWLEDGE	2	5	4	5	5	5	3
6 WIN – LOSE	1	5	5	4	4	4	4
7 TIME CONSUMING – NOT SO	2	4	1	3	2	4	2

FIGURE 40

124

Case No. 3: Trees (pronounced Trace)

This is Trees's analysis:

Constructs

	1	2	3	4	5	6	7
1		−.36	−.26	−.85*	−.34	−.85*	.11
2			.45	.65	.71	.72	.61
3				−.18	.45	.07*	.43
4					.62	.96*	.12
5						.73	.54
6							.17

The numbers marked with an *, are statistically significant. That is, they are not likely to have resulted from chance only.

Here are the results shown graphically:

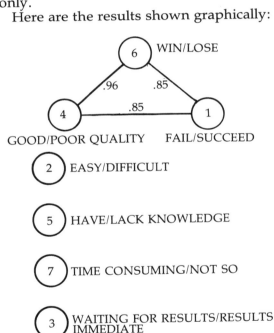

FIGURE 41

So Trees had to work on one cluster and four separate constructs to tackle stress in her work life. As expected failure/success was related to win/lose (the correlation was .85, which means it was likely to be similar but not exactly the same) but construct 4 (good quality) was highly related (.96) to win/lose. This was not so expected.

Trees also looked at the way her elements were related. It is possible to do the same sort of analysis with elements as it is with constructs. By looking at the way elements connect. Trees saw that the internal procedures, new subordinate training, new team working, external liaison and new work schedules all were ranked 4 or 5 by her which meant that she saw them as poor quality and this was related to failure in her eyes.

Looking further, Trees realized that she was new in her job and even during the short time she had been there, changes had been introduced. She had hardly finished her initial training when she had to introduce new ideas she did not fully grasp.

She felt that as a manager she was responsible for their successful implementation, so instead of discussing problems with her boss, Trees fought alone, keeping her problems to herself. This made her even more stressed and she made more mistakes.

A large part of the problem was her reluctance to tell her boss of any problems. She felt she was supposed to be able to cope and consequently should not need help. To ask for help was, in her eyes, a sign of weakness. When her boss asked her if everything was OK, she replied: 'Yes'.

Trees listed her main problems, what especially she found difficult about them and arranged to discuss them with her manager. She also realized that as she was new in the job, she needed a learning period and that during that time she would make mistakes.

Trees also worked on her other stress areas. She started to do some work similar to Jan's about waiting for results but her problems turned out to be different. She was hindered in her work by waiting for other departments to feed her with results of her initial work so that she could progress it further. She decided to tackle this by calling a meeting with other departments to tackle what was a joint problem – not just hers. Like some of the people mentioned, Trees looked at what failure meant to her.

Case No. 4: Wil

Here is Wil's story. He also has one cluster and a few separate constructs.

Constructs

	1	2	3	4	5	6
1		.24	.4	.05	.69	.33
2			.59	.74	.75	.91
3				.48	.53	.58
4					.66	.91*
5						.85*

Again the statistically significant rela- tionships are marked with an *.

Wil's grid is presented graphically in figure 43.

FIGURE 43

REPERTORY GRID FORM

CONSTRUCTS ⟶

ELEMENTS

WIL.

		1	2	3	4	5	6	7
1	SUCCESS UNCERTAIN – DID IT BEFORE	2	3	1	3	3	3	2
2	AMBIGUITY – UNDERSTOOD	2	3	4	5	3	5	3
3	DONT KNOW WHAT I WANT – DO KNOW	3	4	3	4	2	5	1
4	MOTIVATION OF OTHERS IN MY CONTROL – NOT SO	1	3	3	3	1	4	3
5	EMOTIONAL – MECHANISTIC	1	3	1	5	2	5	3
6	NEED TO CONVINCE OTHERS – TECHNICAL ANALYSIS	1	3	3	4	2	5	3

FIGURE 42

The main cluster is all around dealing with other people which to Wil was not straightforward and was ambiguous. Much of his work in tackling stress was looking at how he dealt with others and the meaning of such relationships to him.

It turned out that Wil's difficulty was to get others to carry out unpopular decisions which had been passed down to him by higher management. He didn't like upsetting people. He wanted to be able to get them to do things so that he (Wil) did not feel emotionally affected. He looked at how it was impossible for others not to be angry with some decisions that he expected his subordinates to carry out.

More importantly, Wil looked at how the fact that he was hurt was a measure of his sensitivity to people. Eventually he decided that he wanted to remain the sort of person he was and accept his hurt. Although this is strange it did free Wil from considerable pressure.

Not knowing what he wanted was also a big issue. It was connected with some of the ideas presented about career orientation. Wil had to look at where he wanted to go in his work life. He was torn by an internal image of (1) feeling he had to meet the expectations of his job and (2) his need to do the things he wanted to do. This was a fundamental existential factor in Wil's life. Wil felt better when this conflict was brought into the open. He started to look at it and develop options.

What he eventually decided to do (this was not thought out until much later), was to take early retirement, then start his own business. But meantime he studied so that his new venture was fully prepared by the time he could put it into operation.

Wil also had to look at his construct about 'success uncertain'. His fear of failure was so strong that he tried to get out of things which might fail. This resulted in further problems as unsolved ones surfaced again.

Case No. 5: Frans

This grid includes 'self now' and 'self-like-to-be'.
The analysis shows another variation from what we have seen so far:
Constructs

	1	2	3	4	5	6
1		.32	.87**	.75*	.46	.85**
2			.53	.74*	.52	.47
3				.86*	.75*	.92**
4					.58	.72*
5						.7*

You can see from figure 45, which graphically presents Frans's stress pattern that there is one cluster plus an indirect link (numbers 4 and 2).

Most of Frans's frustration lay around not having a solution to his immediate problems. Looking further, Frans realized that his biggest difficulty was dealing with others. He tended to get overridden at meetings and have to return to his department pushing his people to work with fewer resources compared with other sections.

What Frans needed, above all else, were skills in selling his ideas. He gave up too easily. This went quite deep. He felt that he shouldn't answer back. His way out was through role-playing situations he found difficult and also looking back through his life at other incidents which fitted this pattern.

Frans's correlation between 'self now' and 'self-like-to-be' is +.48. This shows that he has some way to go before he becomes the sort of person he'd like to be but the difference is not impossible. Much of his stress would disappear if he could become more skilled in sticking

REPERTORY GRID FORM

CONSTRUCTS →

ELEMENTS ↓

FRANS

	UNDERSTAFFING	CUSTOMER ACTION	RESOURCE PLANNING	EVALUATION PLANNING	EXTERNAL MTG	STATUS MTG	A+C	SELF NOW	SELF LIKE TO BE
	1	2	3	4	5	6	7	8	9
1 NO MANPOWER – ENOUGH	1	5	4	5	3	5	5	2	4
2 MUST PERSUADE – AUTOMATIC	3	4	4	4	2	4	2	3	5
3 SOLUTION NOT AT HAND – IMMEDIATE	1	5	3	4	3	5	3	2	4
4 EXTRA WORKLOAD – NOT SO	2	5	4	4	2	5	3	3	4
5 PEOPLE RELATED – TECHNICAL	2	3	2	3	3	5	2	2	4
6 NOT CONTROLLABLE – CONTROLLABLE	2	5	4	4	4	5	4	2	5

FIGURE 44

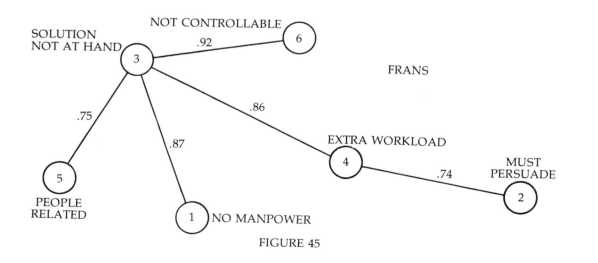

FIGURE 45

with his ideas and not giving in so easily.

From the group of 53 managers from which these five grids were taken there were some commonalities. All shared a major company reorganization and nine mentioned it as one of their stress elements. A few saw it positively, others found it stressful for one reason or another; but the reasons were different. To have attempted a company-wide plan to reduce stress without considering these differences would have left many still with their problems.

TOPIC REFERENCES

Beail, N. (ed.), *Repertory grid techniques and personal constructs*, Croom Helm, 1985.

Fransella, F. and Bannister, D., *A manual for repertory grid techniques*, Academic Press, 1977.

CHAPTER 8

Common work stressors

Although your stressors will be personal to you, it is useful to look at some wider findings as they suggest some helpful action you could take. They will also make you feel that you are not alone.

Common stressors include:

1 Physical working conditions.
2 Work overload.
3 Problems about your work role.

PHYSICAL WORKING CONDITIONS...

Stress can result from adverse physical working conditions. If you work in a coal mine, or as an air traffic controller, in the casualty ward of a hospital, or in a job where you might be called out to deal with urgent repairs in all weathers, or as a shift worker, the physical conditions of your work are dictated by the nature of the job.

Stress is not necessarily and only caused by such external conditions but by the way you see and are able to cope with them. You have to be certain that you are physically and mentally suitable for such work. If you have to remain in an ill-lit environment and you have poor eyesight, your job strain will be that much greater than someone with good eyesight.

Some people are suited to night work, even delight in it, feeling that they are special and liking the freedom it gives as they can do what they want when the rest of the world is at work. Others however, find it difficult to adjust, especially when shifts are changed every few days. Permanent nights suits some, others prefer working long hours for four days and having three days off each week.

If you work in difficult physical conditions which cannot easily be changed or you do not want to, or cannot change your job, there are some things you can do to help matters:

1 Learn to relax. Practise every day, making it part of your daily routine.
2 Develop interests that compensate for the sort of work you do.
3 Take up a physically satisfying hobby or sport.
4 Take care of what you eat, reduce intake of meat and animal fat, do not drink heavily and reduce, or better still, cut out smoking. Watch your weight but beware of crash diets.

WORK OVERLOAD

Work overload can be temporary. There is a rush of unexpected work, or someone has left your department. If you can see a definite time limit, a heavy work load is bearable. You can stick it out.

More serious is the problem when you cannot see an end to your hours of heavy burden.

You need to examine how your workload compares with others doing a similar job. The problem may be in the departmental work load itself or how the work is allocated but if others seem to cope the problem needs to be tackled at an individual level.

There are different types of overload:

quantity too much
quality standards too demanding
complexity too difficult for you
variety and changes disrupt your work patterns

These points need to be dealt with differently.

Some of us find certain work easy, for others it is a strain. You may be in the wrong job or need training to help you cope with some of the more difficult aspects of your work. Some people, for instance, take hours to write a report, others only minutes. Training improves your skill.

Suitability for a job involves a complex mixture of:

personality traits
aptitudes
skills
intelligence
physical qualities
your own interests

Even with the right mixture you still need training. Usually it is not the whole job which is unsuitable but just some aspects of it. It may be possible to modify these parts or for you to improve your skills in dealing with them.

If you break your job into different tasks and apply a Work Study approach, you may be able to modify what you do sufficiently to reduce some of the overload.

Here's how you go about a simplified work study analysis – you ask a series of questions:

1 WHAT is being done? What are the end results? Can these be measured? Is output increasing or decreasing?

Then challenge what is being done. Does it need to be done at all? Is every aspect necessary? What do the end users do with it? What would happen if they never received it?

Can it – or part of it – be eliminated?

2 WHY is it done at that time? Could it be done later, earlier, less frequently? Are the cycle and sequence right? Could part of the cycle be eliminated, modified or merged? If there are bottlenecks, what could be done to reduce them? What are major holdups? What interrupts you from doing what you need to do? Analyse your interruptions. These can be a major source of delay.

3 WHERE is it done? Why that place? Could it more easily be done elsewhere? Could it be done locally, centrally, or combined with a previous stage?

4 WHO does it? Why that person? Who else could do it? If you have people working for you, do consider delegation.

5 HOW is it done? Why that method? How could the process be improved? Could it be simplified or mechanized? There are many systems and procedures available which speed up administrative work.

What aspects of the job cause you major problems?

In some cases it is useful to look at the whole system. You can be caught in a trap of an increasingly efficient bureaucracy.

As office technology advances, especially with more and more powerful computers, bureaucracy *in theory* becomes more effective. Management information systems operate more sensitively, more widely and more quickly.

Senior managers have control information within days, whereas in the past they had to wait months before they knew that things had gone wrong and then it was often too late to do anything about it!

Such improved systems have their adverse side – especially as far as human beings are concerned. When overloaded we usually prioritize our work by selecting only more urgent work – leaving less pressing tasks to do only if we have time. A modern management information system soon picks up the work we leave and puts pressure on us to get it done. We feel forced to change our priorities and to start and discard other work. The system then catches up with us once again – noting the new unfinished tasks – and so on until eventually we feel forced to attempt everything.

To do this, we trade quality against quantity. We meet our target but quality falls.

The system, however, notes the fall in quality and we are informed. If the problem is widespread the company introduces quality control circles, campaigns, drives and other activities designed to impress on us the importance of good quality. If they work, we begin to feel guilty about the standards of what we produce. If the activities are really effective, we become enthusiastic. We return to our work place determined to improve things.

The trap is now tighter, we are forced to produce results *and* at the quality required. This we find almost impossible so our next fall back is to reduce the time we spend with people, coaching, training and motivating them. Our subordinates are seen less frequently. We are too pressed to deal with potential problems. Our ever-open door has a clear but unwritten message on it: 'keep out'.

It is not that easy, for a good management information system goes further than quantity and quality. It also measures morale. Attitude surveys start to show that morale is declining. Senior management are alerted. Further surveys and interviews are conducted to get at the heart of the problem. Results: a rush of motivation and man-management courses. We are reminded that people are the company's most important asset. Senior managers hold meetings to impress on us that the company expects us to be people managers first and foremost. The managing director appears on videos with the same message. We are convinced and begin to pay more attention to those who work for us.

The trap is now complete. We must produce results – quantity and quality *and* care for people.

We learn to survive by looking for the weak points in the organization; managers who do not follow things through find their requests ignored. We meet only the demands of the strong and persistent.

The energy we put into playing this game, reduces what we have available to do our job. We find things catch up on us. We make promises we can't keep. We begin to feel stressed and this further reduces our capacity to work effectively. We work on the assumption that the company's demands are legitimate and that we should meet them. We find that we do not have the resources but we still feel obliged to try. Our stress is socially created by the way we legitimize our organization's demands. It is also a way out for us. We put in more time and energy until we become too ill to cope. It is as if stress has been created as a socially acceptable way out of our impossible dilemma.

There are positive things we could do. First is to understand where we are and the reason for it. Next we can set priorities and then negotiate these with our manager. He or she has to know clearly what we intend to concentrate on, and what will be left undone if necessary and the consequences of so doing. We have to help force him or her to face the realities of the situation. We can do more and take the initiative and see how widespread are these problems in the company. If they are widespread we can suggest a project meeting to discuss and attempt to resolve them. We are not trying to make the company less efficient. In fact exactly the opposite. We are getting it to face facts and stop playing a game.

When we present proposals we need to be sure of our facts and quantify them where possible. We have to show that the work load is still increasing and to what extent. We need to be able to prove the adverse effects of attempting too much. Just to complain is insufficient.

Sometimes we have to look deeper – inside ourselves. It is not that the work load is too high but that we create pressures because that's how we need to operate.

In Transactional Analysis, there is a psychological game called 'harried'. It is a game played by some – but not all – type A personalities. Players take on more than they can cope with, creating excessive work pressure. They pile work upon work. 'Yes' is their stock reply to requests. Their activities have to be seen to be well above the rest of the employees. They remain working during the lunch break, stay late at night, attend all meetings, take work home with them, call into the office at weekends.

They certainly get recognized. Senior managers reinforce their behaviour. For the price of one executive, you get the output of two! Such work commitment earns promotion. Their excessive effort is held up as an example to others. They are driven to work hard. The push is within.

In reality, their efficiency only appears high. They are unable to delegate effectively; either trying to do everything themselves or delegating too much to their subordinates. They become the victims of stress with all related physical ailments – heart disease, ulcers etc. When they depart – often through illness, they leave behind them a power vacuum. There is nobody like them to take over.

Why do they do it? In Transactional Analysis theory there are four existential positions in life.
These are:

I am OK/ you are OK
I am OK/ you are not OK
I am not OK/ you are not OK
I am not OK/ you are OK

This, perhaps somewhat crude categorization, summarizes relationships with ourselves and with others.

In the first category: 'I am OK/you are OK', you feel fairly good about yourself most of the time and see others in the same way. You have a healthy, positive regard for yourself and for other people.

The second is an elitist view. You are OK but others are not, they need to be told what to do, to be supervised and checked up on. They are essentially lazy and generally irresponsible. You look down on them. They are not really to be trusted. To obtain satisfactory results you need to do things yourself. You are authoritarian. You believe that others do not want, and indeed are not capable of, responsibility.

One difficulty of this life-orientation is that it becomes self-fulfilling. If you don't give responsibility to others, they become demotivated. They start to dislike their work. You then have to start pushing and checking on their activities.

The worst combination is the third one: no one, including yourself, you feel, is much use. It is all pretty hopeless. At its most severe, you want to finish it all.

The final category is the basis for the 'harried' playing executive. You feel somehow that you are not OK but other people are. They always seem to get things done and they appear competent. They seem to have inner qualities that you feel you are denied. You feel inwardly as if you are not much use. You try to hide this basic feeling about yourself by putting on a front of being super-efficient, showing the world that you can tackle more than anybody else. You need others to recognize that you are 'special'. The way you do it is to work so damn hard that others have to see you this way.

Once you've got into this way of behaving, it is difficult to get out of it. It becomes a way of life. It doesn't alter how you feel inwardly; that's why you have to keep it up.

The way out is to recognize the pattern and that you are attempting to hide a myth. You are working so hard to show that you are OK but you will never prove it to yourself this way. The answer lies in an inner realization that you don't have to prove yourself.

Try this laddering exercise. Ask yourself this question:

'Why is it important to me to have to appear to other people as someone special?'

You might reply:

'Because underneath, I am nobody.'

If you reach this level quickly, ask yourself what it means to be a somebody. You might answer that this is the only way to obtain respect.

Dig deeper by elaborating what you mean by respect. You might find that what you are doing is to get them to validate your essential worth as a person. Now spend some time considering whether people actually do value others in this way.

As you work through this exercise, you may find that thoughts and memories about past failures flood into your mind. Look again at those 'failures'. How would someone else describe them? What did you do about them? What would it have been like if you had not had any of them? Maybe they forced you to improve yourself – so you have gained something out of them. How threatening would it be if you were kinder and more forgiving to yourself.

Other people push themselves for different reasons. The actual causes don't matter overmuch, except to help you examine the full extent of your behaviour.

You have to be careful that you do not 'slot rattle'. 'Slot rattling' describes behaviour where you move from one pole of a construct to the other. You replace your driving energy with lethargy. The alternative is not usually effective. It is not likely to satisfy you either and you find that you revert to your old ways after a short break.

It is not that what you do is always negative, sometimes there is a time for drive, energy and even toughness. But there is also a need to set priorities, delegate, give yourself time to think, consider longer term and wider issues and develop positive personal relationships with people. There is also a time for rest, fun and for a complete break from work. You need to learn to pace yourself and to relax.

You have to be careful that you don't tackle your stress reduction programme in the same way as your job, by planning, setting targets for relaxation proficiency and organizing your breaks at exactly the correct time and duration. Relaxation means giving in and letting go. You cannot organize it like a production schedule.

Sometimes the problem of overload is because you are uncertain about what is expected of you. You are never sure that what you produce is totally correct and sufficient. You try harder but still remain uncertain.

You delay action because you know that you are responsible if things go wrong. So your work piles up. You always seem to be trying to catch up. Your last minute decisions, forced now by time pressure, lack the care and thought of decisions developed in calmer circumstances. You might even ensure that you are so busy that you do not have time to face other and more important issues or to give you a ready-made excuse for failure.

Even with a good track record you can feel uncertain. Your anticipation that your success record will be broken lies at the back of your mind – reminding you of your fallibility.

Reconstruing 'failure' might help. There are two sorts of mistakes. Those of principle suggest that you do not fully understand part of the job. For this you need training.

Sometimes you may not be suited to your work. You may have been promoted to your level of incompetence as the 'Peter Principle' suggests. This says that managers tend to get promoted until they reach a level at which they are incompetent and then stay there. Your previous work record warranted promotion. Now it does not. This is where you remain. Just about coping.

If you seriously feel that this applies to you, discuss the problem with your manager or personnel department. Initiate a sideways move or even ask for a less responsible job. Examine assumptions about always having to move upwards and that self-worth is embedded in being upwardly mobile. Listen to what your stress is saying to you. It may be shouting at you about taking it easy. I know one personnel director who recommended his own demotion. He had the courage and sense to move out of a position which he could just about fulfil to one that he felt on top of. As he said to me 'What do you think life is about?'

An exercise: try letting your stress talk to you. I know this seems silly. But try it. Imagine that your stress was a person. What would this person say to you? It might be something like this:

'You push yourself and do things that don't suit you. You force yourself to accept standards that are impossible. You coerce, kick and push yourself into living a life you dislike. You force yourself to travel daily to face friction which is usually generated by you. You make our work place a battle. You are wearing yourself out. You are really fed up with fighting. I am trying to protect you. I send you warning signals to show that all is not well. But you won't listen, so I have to make the signals stronger.'

The other sort of errors are those of detail, often due to too much work, or doing more than one thing at a time. When your mental processing system is overloaded it breaks down. You forget things. You make mistakes – even developing 'tunnel vision' where you can only concentrate on one immediate task, ignoring all else. You miss important things that are not your immediate concern.

PROBLEMS ABOUT YOUR WORK ROLE

Role is a powerful aspect of your job. Roles are about power and influence. They are about ways in which you are expected to behave.

Consider these problems:

1 Role conflict – you are torn between different demands which are difficult to reconcile. For instance, as a junior

member of a management group, you feel responsible to that group. As a manager, you are also concerned with the people who report to you. You might belong to a professional society, to a trade union, be a staff representative on your company's consultative committee. The more conscientious you are, the more sensitive you will be to the pressures that these conflicting roles create.

Sometimes the problem centres around having to work for – and satisfy – more than one boss.

Sometimes it is even more complex. Your management group wants to push through ideas which, although financially advantageous, will demotivate your team. You sense that the company is cutting corners. This conflicts with the high standards advocated by your professional society and which you personally feel are right.

As part of the new proposals, one of your subordinates is to be eased out. He feels he is being unfairly treated. So do you. His trade union has already protested to the company. You've been told to oppose them but pretend to go along with them and say you will investigate the matter but do not take any action.

The case is to be raised at the next consultative committee. To make it more complicated, your own boss is not too keen on some of the new proposals and he's asked you to try to delay things and give him some inside information which more senior managers have given you in confidence. Senior management are keen to make rapid progress. They expect your support. They've hinted that your next promotion depends on it.

You are pushed in many directions. Objective decision making seems inadequate to help you select the best course of action. You find, to your surprise and disgust, that you are agreeing with whatever person or group you're with.

You begin to feel guilty about this – you are not the open, honest, fair person you thought you were.

Jessie is asked to write a report which 'objectively' outlines advantages and disadvantages of a new work practice. Her boss makes it pretty clear that she favours one particular alternative and expects Jessie to slant the facts to fit. This is not spelt out but the message is clear.

Barry has spent months working on a research project. He presents his findings but is asked to 'clean up' his report by not cluttering it up with exceptions and possible adverse side effects. Barry feels that these need to be stated. This is the third time he's fought over such issues. At his last appraisal, he was reminded about the need for company loyalty. He was also warned about getting the reputation of a rebel.

Doreen is a nurse in a private hospital and has been told that she must be responsible for cutting costs so that the organization maximizes its profits. Her views are that more should be spent because patients need it. She feels she is there to care for patients not to maximize profits. She is certain there is very little wastage anyway.

There are no easy answers to these dilemmas of role conflict. There are no straight cut moral rule books to which you can refer. You can search your conscience but sometimes the message is unclear and what your conscience genuinely tells you may be quite different from the consciences of others. If we each refer to our conscience, each may receive a different message. Many of the major battles in history have been fought by armies each of whom felt that their cause was just and that God was on their side.

Even if you feel morality is objective, that is intrinsically embedded in each situation, that situations are objectively good or evil, others will perceive a different 'objectivity'.

The utilitarian argument doesn't help much either. The problem with the greatest good for the greatest number is who decides what is best and what about minorities?

You may feel history indicates right action (a key part of Marxist philosophy) but even here there are deep debates about what history actually teaches us. What seems so right in one decade now appears immoral.

Perhaps the only practical approach is to look upon our beliefs as tentative, test them out and be prepared to modify them. We can also try putting ourselves in the shoes of others and subsuming their views. This may not stop us doing things but at least we realize how others will be affected.

Some of us try to sidestep such problems and aim for friendly, harmonious surface relationships. We leave tensions, hostility and suspicions simmering underneath – unresolved.

Others agree with what's being asked and carry out instructions under silent protest. They remind themselves that they are not really part of the set up.

Open rebellion is another, but more dangerous, approach. Many who have tried it have found their careers finished. In a survey in the United States of fifty-five employees who opposed their organization for reasons of ethics, all paid a great personal price. One commented, about advising others what to do: 'Forget it'; another said: 'If you have God, the law, the press and the facts on your side, you have a 50–50 chance of winning'. Some, however, found the experience rewarding.

In some professions there are public expectations. Doctors, nurses, paramedics, teachers, police, firemen, the armed services and others find that their roles are prescribed by the society.

This public image expects high standards. These are reinforced by professional pressures. We have internalized these values and feel that we must meet them. There are also external sanctions for the deviant. Doctors, as they progress through medical school, as well as acquiring skills, are socialized into accepting values connected with their profession.

Nurses are confronted with pain and death. They are responsible for people's lives. Internal pressure to live up to ideals about what they think the public expect of them is great. In practice they realize that limited resources within the health service and also within themselves make it impossible to do what they consider should be done. They begin to feel personally inadequate.

Emotions push them towards being sympathetic but their time is limited – they must get the job done. Some have unresolved anxieties about their own death and this makes it difficult to deal with dying patients.

Some depersonalize their behaviour, cutting themselves off from the human side of their work. They cannot afford to suffer with the patient. They cannot spend time listening to a patient who needs to talk or gently tell someone that they are dying and stay with them. Some sense the suffering of others and are aware of their own lack of compassion, which was their reason for taking up nursing in the first place. Where their work meta-theme was one of work as a vocation, conflict is considerable.

In one study in the USA, nurses looking after the terminally ill could not cope with the demands of all those who needed help, so they developed priorities based upon 'loss differentials' – that is the value they felt the patient had as a person. Their attention was allocated in this way.

These internal stereotypes that we have about what society expects of us are not limited to work. Expectations connected with being 'a good mother', always feeling caring, loving and having endless resources to amuse, contrast starkly with how we actually feel and what we do. Sometimes we are too tired. We are bad tempered. We promise to try even harder, even if we have to deny our own needs. Our failures then seem even greater.

Take a look at such public stereotyping. Examine the impossibility of being perfect. Consider your needs as well as those of others.

2 Role ambiguity – you're not quite certain what's expected of you. This differs from role conflict, where what is expected is all too clear.

Ambiguity in a new job is usual. It takes a few weeks to know what's what. When you are promoted you also need time to settle in.

For some, this uncertainty remains. Their stress is not dramatic. It is the daily feeling of not quite knowing what's expected. The reason may be external – clear information is lacking. Your objectives are vague, your authority unclear, you only know that you are responsible for results. Managers in such situations have lower job satisfaction, are more tense and lack self-confidence.

You might try defining your own objectives and authority and presenting these to your boss, telling him or her that this is how you are going to perform unless you're told otherwise. You call their bluff. If you are uncertain, write down exactly what you are uncertain about, note what you think you should be doing and check it out.

Another cause is internal, within you. Your job is clearly defined but you fail to trust yourself about how you should perform. You continually doubt, starting along one path and then changing your mind. Doubt has some value, it keeps your options open but the problem is, if you keep them open too long, you are too late. You also have to live with the fact that you can never be 100% certain. You have to make decisions on limited evidence and you do not have time to collect all the facts. Life is not like that.

Here is a grid to help you examine some of your problems connected with role.

The elements are:

1 Me now as a person.
2 Me as I would like to be.
3 Me as my clients (eg students, patients or whatever is appropriate) expect me to be.
4 Me as my professional association expects me to be.
5 Me as the administration of my organization expect me to be.
6 Me as my professional superiors expect me to be.
7 Me as I feel society expects me to be.
8 Me as the ideal........ (add your profession here).
9 The inadequate........ (nurse, doctor, lawyer etc) (add your profession here).

You may need to modify some of the questions slightly to fit your particular case.

Select combinations as you have done with earlier grids:

1	1 2 3
2	4 5 6
3	7 8 9
4	1 4 7
5	2 5 8
6	3 6 9
7	1 5 9
8	2 3 4
9	6 7 8

List the emergent constructs on the grid role form.

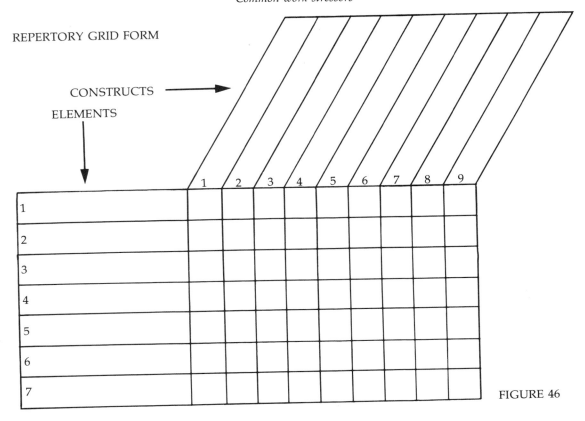

REPERTORY GRID FORM

CONSTRUCTS ⟶

ELEMENTS

FIGURE 46

Follow the instructions for previous grid analyses.

Here are some constructs which emerged with one client:

1 Cut corners ←→ professional service
2 Competent ←→ only here for the money
3 Bewildered ←→ has all the answers
4 More people orientated ←→ technically orientated
5 Resourceful ←→ inadequate
6 Giving support ←→ needing support
7 Creative ←→ play safe
8 Innovative ←→ static

Take a look at how 'me-now-as-a-person' fits in with these constructs. Then consider 'me-as-I-would-like-to-be'. Check that this is how you would really like to be and is not what you feel society or your profession expects you to be. If you do a correlation analysis, see how closely these two elements fit, that is how closely related to where you want to be. If the correlation is negative, this means that you are quite different from how you'd like to be. Have a look at what's pushing you to be that sort of person.

A way that can be helpful is to take part in a Transactional Analysis life script mentioned in chapter 3 and see what messages from childhood still govern your present-day world of work. If you have not tried the exercise, do so now and see where it leads. You may gain insights which show how many of your stresses are due to attempting to live in an adult world with out-of-date messages from childhood.

TOPIC REFERENCES

Organizational Structures:
Likert, R., *The patterns of management*, McGraw-Hill, 1961.

Cross Cultural Studies:
Hofstede, G., 'Motivation, leadership, organizations' in *Organizational Dynamics*, 1980.

Repertory Grids:
Fransella, F. and Bannister, D., *A manual of repertory grid techniques*, Academic Press, 1977.

Work Study:
Introducing Work Study, International Labour Office, 1964.

Moral Dilemmas:
Lessnoff, M., *The structure of social science*, George Allen and Unwin, 1974.

Nurses and loss differentials:
Glaser, B. C., 'The constant comparative method of qualitative analysis' in *Issues in participant observation*, McCall Simmon, 1969.

CHAPTER 9

Right job, no job, new job

You have looked at stress connected with work but one important aspect is whether you are in the right job in the first place? Or that you have a job at all.

This does not mean that if you feel that your job is not right for you, you should necessarily change it. That may not be possible.

This section aims to help you look a little closer at the sort of work you'd find fulfilling.

This is best done after you've considered meta-orientations to work. You may not just be dissatisfied with your job but with the whole idea of tying yourself to a career. Look at this first.

The process is a loosening and tightening exercise. You open up your mind, exploring ideas and then tighten so that you can examine their feasibility and plan practical action. Repeat the cycle until you know where your preferences lie and what you can do about them.

A good start is to work through a repertory grid. The method will not be explained in detail because you should by now have become quite proficient in completing grids! If you have any doubts, return to the earlier examples for a fuller explanation.

Here are the questions to help you select your elements. Write these on the grid form (figure 47):

1 Think of a work activity that you really like doing.

Place this element in the first element column on the grid form.

2 Select another work activity which you would (or do) dislike doing.

Place in the second column of the grid form.

3 Now select another element similiar to number 1.

Place in column 3.

4 Select a routine work activity which, although not so fulfilling, you quite enjoy doing. Label and place in column 4.

5 Select a routine work event which you do not (or feel you would not) like doing. Label and place in column 5.

6 Select another work activity which you have never done but you feel you would enjoy doing. Label and place in column 6.

7 If you had the choice of any sort of work, what would it be? Label and place in column 7.

8 Name a job which you would really hate doing; what would be the worst sort of work for you.

Place it in column number 8.

9 If you haven't used it yet, write in your present job. If you have used it then place in column 9 any previous job you've done, not already mentioned.

You should have a list of nine elements.

Make your first selection of three elements and note which two go together and which is the odd one out.

As with the previous examples, you

REPERTORY GRID FORM

CONSTRUCTS →

ELEMENTS ↓

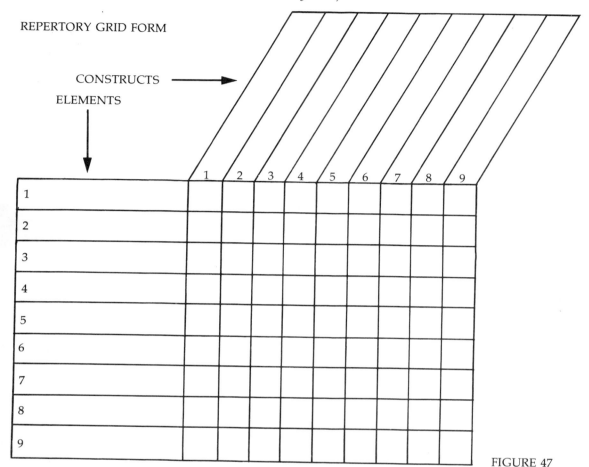

FIGURE 47

work through various combinations of triads.

Here is the order of selection:

123
456
789
147
258
369
159
367
248

Start with elements 1, 2, and 3. Ask yourself which two are more similar and what it is that makes them similar. Ex-

clude superficial similarities.

Your selection provides you with constructs. Your previous constructs were directly connected with stress, here they are about work satisfaction. You can compare them with earlier ones and see how they link.

When you have obtained your first construct, consider its opposite. Again, like your earlier constructs, this may not be the dictionary opposite.

Write your first construct – both its positive and opposite poles in the first row of the construct section, place the positive pole in the left-hand column. This makes it easier for you to analyse

142

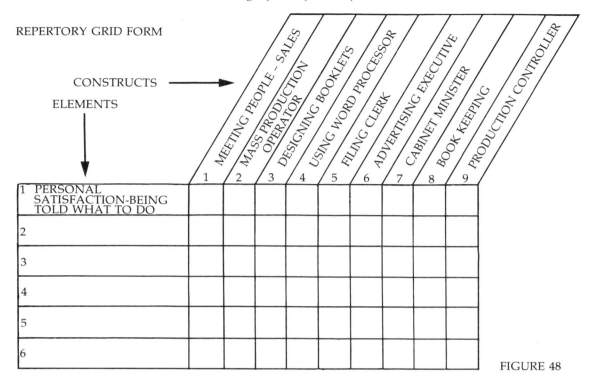

REPERTORY GRID FORM

CONSTRUCTS ⟶

ELEMENTS

	MEETING PEOPLE – SALES	MASS PRODUCTION OPERATOR	DESIGNING BOOKLETS	USING WORD PROCESSOR	FILING CLERK	ADVERTISING EXECUTIVE	CABINET MINISTER	BOOK KEEPING	PRODUCTION CONTROLLER
	1	2	3	4	5	6	7	8	9
1 PERSONAL SATISFACTION-BEING TOLD WHAT TO DO									
2									
3									
4									
5									
6									

FIGURE 48

your results without a computer. If you do a more complex computer analysis, it doesn't matter where you place the positive or negative poles. See the example in figure 48.

Now continue with the remainder of the triads. You should end up with a list of nine constructs, each with their positive and negative poles. If you cannot obtain nine, do not worry, work with whatever number you are able to get. If you think of more than nine, that's fine – just add a few more rows to the construct section of the form. Try to obtain different constructs from each triad.

The next stage is for you to grade all the elements so that they reflect the way they fit your constructs. Use a 1 to 5 grading system. Where the left-hand pole of a construct fits exactly with an element, allocate 5 points; where it fits, but somewhat less so, allocate 4 points.

Where it is the exact opposite (it fits the right-hand pole of the construct), allocate 1 point, with other points in between:

left-hand pole   right-hand pole
degree of correspondence
1   2   3   4   5

Figure 49 shows an example.

The next stage is to check through to see which rows fit with which other rows, as you did previously.

You can either attempt to match the lines visually, or you can copy out the first line and move it along each of the other rows, comparing it with the second, third, forth and subsequent rows. Then do the same with the second row, comparing it with rows three, four, five and six and so on.

What you are doing is to:

REPERTORY GRID FORM

CONSTRUCTS ⟶

ELEMENTS

		1 MEETING PEOPLE – SALES	2 MASS PRODUCTION OPERATOR	3 DESIGNING BOOKLETS	4 USING WORD PROCESSOR	5 FILING CLERK	6 ADVERTISING EXECUTIVE	7 CABINET MINISTER	8 BOOK KEEPING	9 PRODUCTION CONTROLLER
1	PERSONAL SATISFACTION – BEING TOLD WHAT TO DO	1	5	2	3	4	2	1	5	3
2	DEALING WITH PEOPLE – MECHANISTIC	1	4	2	3	3	1	2	4	3
3	PERSONAL DEVELOPMENT – STATIC	2	5	3	3	5	2	1	5	3
4	NEW – ROUTINE	2	5	1	3	5	1	1	5	3
5	CREATIVE – DULL	2	5	1	3	5	1	2	5	4
6	HAPPY – STRESSED	1	5	2	3	5	1	2	5	4
7	CONTACT – ALONE	1	5	3	4	3	1	2	4	2
8	QUALITY IMPORTANT – ANYTHING GOES	3	3	1	2	3	2	2	1	2
9	RESPONSIBILITY – NONE	2	5	2	2	4	2	1	2	2

FIGURE 49

compare line 1 with lines 2, 3, 4 5, 6, 7, 8 and 9

compare line 2 with lines 3, 4, 5, 6, 7, 8 and 9

compare line 3 with lines 4, 5, 6, 7, 8 and 9

and so on with the remaining lines. This will show how your constructs form sub-systems.

You can take it that rows are similar if they are exactly the same or only have two or three points different.

constructs	1	2	3	4	5	6	7	8	9
1		.9**	.95**	.92**	.87**	.9*	.8**	.01	.69*
2			.81**	.85**	.88**	.92**	.88**	− .1	.52
3				.92**	.84**	.84**	.75*	.1	.76*
4					.97**	.94**	.7*	.3	.71*
5						.98**	.65	.3	.63
6							.7*	.2	.62
7								− .1	.57
8									.59

The easiest way is to use a computer to do a principal or factor analysis program. This provides a print out similar to the one above which shows the relationships between the repertory grid in figure 49:

Just by looking at the figures, you can see a large number of '*'s. This means that relationships are not likely to have occurred by chance. You can also see that the figures are quite high. This indicates that links between the constructs are also high.

A principal component analysis shows that, in this example, there is only one main component and that every other construct is linked to it, except number 8 – 'Quality important'. The principal component is number 4 – 'New'.

You can see this clearly in figure 50.

The idea of working in an environment where there are lots of new tasks is important here. It means being happy, unstressed, creative and feeling responsible. Contact with people is also connected with it. The price paid for a job without this possibility would be to feel dull and be stressed.

Elements (that is the actual jobs) can also be analysed in the same way. Figure 51 shows the relationship between the various jobs.

You can see that there is one main cluster around 'bookkeeping' plus two indirect links: 'filing clerk' and 'meeting people' The last one is linked negatively (− .69) to 'word processing'.

It looks as if jobs are divided into 'people' and 'task' categories. The present job

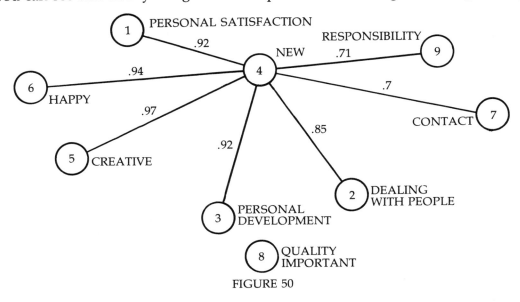

FIGURE 50

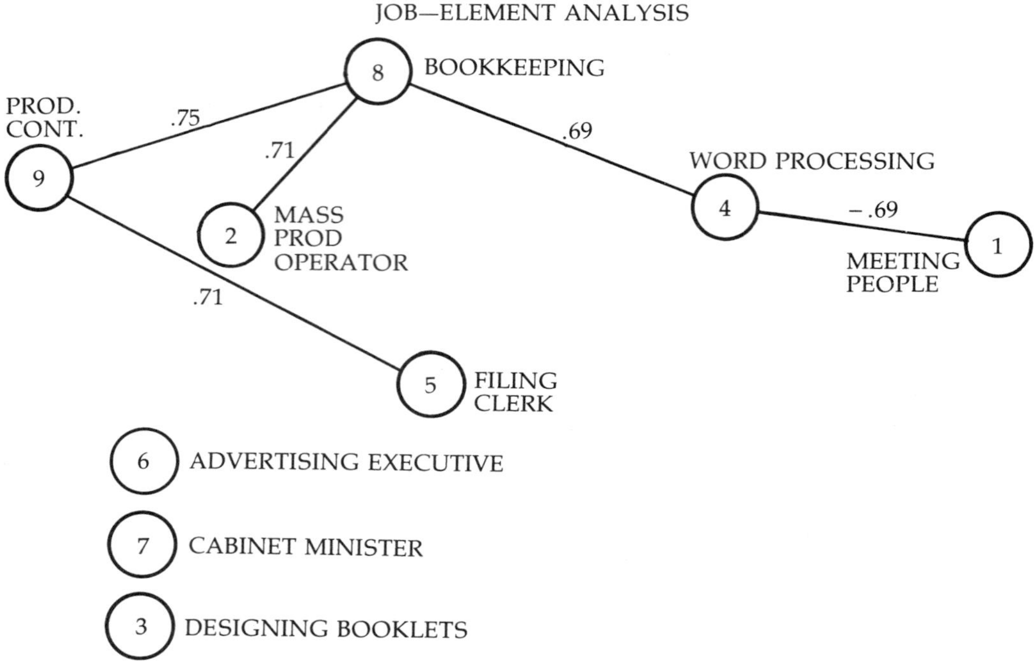

JOB—ELEMENT ANALYSIS

FIGURE 51

is related to 'bookkeeping' and 'filing clerk'.

This is the start of the journey.

Whatever method you use, draw the structure of your constructs and if possible your elements as well.

WORKING OUT WHAT IT MEANS ...

Look through your grid. Note where constructs are linked. They indicate what you are looking for in a job. You may be seeking the routine which is safe and secure; or perhaps your need is to be with people – or to get away from them. Nothing is right and nothing is wrong. These are your needs. Listen to what you are saying to yourself – for that is what the information on your grid is about.

Try a laddering exercise about clusters of constructs. First give the cluster a new construct name which you feel represents

a collective title for it.

Laddering will show you why the cluster is important to you.

Next, write a description of what you want out of work, using information from the laddering exercise and the original constructs. Write in the third person.

This is an example taken from information in the previous grid (figure 49):

'Joe Smith is looking for personal satisfaction in work and he seems to think he will find it through a job where he has frequent contact with people. He is also concerned with personal development, so needs an organization which provides opportunities for training courses and has career prospects.

'He likes creative work and wants to take responsibility for what he does.

'Joe gives cabinet minister as his fantasy job. Laddering showed that he'd like this because of its prestige, recognition and a chance to do something worthwhile. This led him to consider how im-

146

portant it was for him to feel that the efforts he put into his work were of value. He had considered advertising as personally satisfying, giving him plenty of contact with people, offering new challenges, being creative and also providing responsibility but somehow this worries Joe. He is concerned about its worthwhileness. He would not like to work on products he feels are harmful – for example, cigarettes.

'Joe wants to get out of the line that he is in at present (production control). It is uncreative, dull, quite stressful and he has little contact with people. It is also fairly routine. He knows that he has made a big mistake in taking that sort of work.

'Joe's thoughts seem to be crystallizing around working for a charity and within this, helping with public relations and advertising...'

Just let the ideas flow so that the script almost writes itself. Analyse what you've written. See how your preferences fit into the following categories:

active, outdoor work
social, dealing with people
creative
numeric (eg accounting, computing)
intellectual
scientific
literary

Read through newspaper advertisements in the jobs vacant section. Mark those you'd like doing in red and those you would dislike in blue. Make a list of your likes and dislikes. Analyse your list, for example:

LIKE	DISLIKE
prestige	poor pay
meeting people	working alone
creativity	tied to a desk
etc	etc

As you work through these exercises, it should become more and more clear what you'd really like to do. Try to include a number of possibilities.

Take a look at the patterns which have emerged from your work grid. Ponder over what constructs are important to you. List and weight them: 5 for very important and 1 for not so important.

Place this figure in the first column of the form below. Then weight how strongly you feel that particular need is met in your present job, using a smaller scale. (That is 5 fully met, 1 hardly met at all.) Place this figure in the second column. Multiply these two figures and put your answer in the last column.

Construct	importance weighting (5–1)	degree of present satisfaction	total points
interesting work	4	3	12
using my skills	5	1	5
being creative	4	2	8
quality work	5	4	20
people contact	5	1	5
responsibility	4	2	8
innovative work	5	1	5
learning something new	4	2	8
recognition	4	2	8
total	40	satisfaction total score	79

Your job satisfaction form

Motivation construct	importance weighting 5–1	degree present in existing job 5–1
1		
2		
3		
4		
5		
6		
7		
8		
totals		

Here is an example followed by an uncompleted form for your use.

If you multiply the total in the first column by 5, you get the total number of points for complete satisfaction (200 in this example). You can then compare your total satisfaction score with it.

In this example there are 79 points out of a total of 200. The job provides about forty per cent satisfaction.

If your score is low, you need to ask yourself how important work is to you. Look at how it fits in with the rest of your life. Your job might be relatively boring but the rest of your life full of interest and satisfaction. This is fine. You've got a good balance.

You can do a similar exercise for potential jobs. Grade how satisfactory you think they would be. If you have a number of possibilities in mind, your gradings will help you make a choice.

Be creative. Do not be limited by conventional career pathways. Look at the various orientations to work mentioned in a previous chapter. Consider self-employment, part-time work, working in a co-operative, temporary work, work outside the UK, job sharing, even voluntary work if you have sufficient to live on.

You might also think of a dual career, for example working in an office and also developing your talent as a writer.

If you are returning to work after a number of years looking after your children, you may doubt your abilities, be worried about how you will cope and feel out of the run of the work world. Some married women have told me that it has taken them over a year to get enough courage to take the first step of finding out what is available. The barriers are inside you. You have to act even though you are afraid.

You now have to look at what you have to offer: your personal qualities, background, training, skills and experience. Next consider your limitations. Your aptitudes, skills, education and experience may not match your job preferences. You need to see what practical steps you could take to bridge the gap. Design a practical plan. Include alternative goals as well as ways to reach them.

Look at the pressures which hinder you getting what you want. And then at the factors which aid you. Draw them. Put the positive ones at the top and the negative ones at the bottom. Make the

148

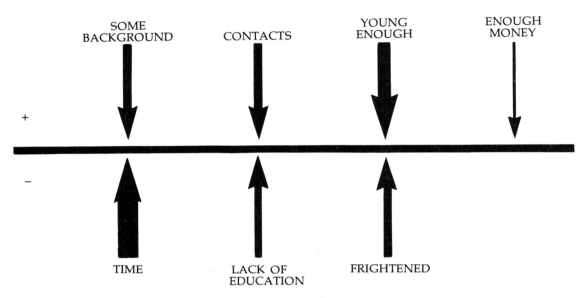

FIGURE 52

thickness of the arrows suggest their respective strengths.

Next work out steps you need to take to strengthen the positive points and overcome the negative ones.

In getting a job, search the local and national press and reply to advertisements; use employment agencies; ask around friends and other contacts you know: try recruitment and similar agencies or make direct approaches to potential employers.

Your local reference library will help with publications giving the names and addresses of major firms. Do some research before you start. You do need to be persistent. It can take hundreds of approaches before success. Think out what your prospective employer would like from you.

Write short, clear, neat and straight-to-the-point letters of application. Get your letter typed. If you have considerable experience, send a short covering letter and curriculum vitae on a separate sheet. The aim of your letter is not to get the job but to get an interview.

CHAPTER 10

Making yourself more effective at work

Your grid analysis has helped you pinpoint stress problems connected with your job. You have looked at how career orientation, role ambiguity and conflict, and the relationship between home and work can add to stress in your life. You have seen how organizational bureaucracy can, by monitoring your performance, trap you into striving for a theoretically optimum performance.

You have seen that there are many ways of perceiving situations and that these new insights can lead to constructive problem-solving and action. Looking at circumstances from different angles can unfreeze you. You begin to feel that you are in control once more. Your analysis may have shown how you, yourself, create tensions by seeking out pressures, through overloading yourself by accepting too much work.

When you have cleared away all these points, you can then move on to making yourself more effective in the actual tasks you carry out in your job. By increasing your competence, you further reduce stress and increase control.

Speeding up report writing, managing your time more usefully, preparing more quickly and actually giving better presentations and improving your decision making skills can help you get on top of your job. You have more time to think and your work becomes more fulfilling and interesting. Instead of dreading work days, you start to enjoy them.

This section is mainly for managers and supervisors. Others may also find some of the ideas useful. Trades Unionists, members of works councils, those who run clubs and associations should be able to extract useful ways to improve their skills. Even if you work at home as a housewife, you may find the sections on people skills and decision making some help.

It is important that you tackle underlying causes first. If you were ill and needed hospital treatment, it doesn't help taking up physical fitness training until your ailment has been cured. It doesn't help to improve your theoretical decision-making skills only to find that you have a psychological barrier about making decisions. This is what was meant by 'unfreezing' energies first.

There are three main areas in which you could consider improving your competence:

1 Communications skills.
2 People skills.
3 Decision making.

For each we will consider specific and practical ways which might help you. Each section offers a package of basic skills. From these you can take the ideas further by attending courses, reading books or other learning material. Do not try to tackle too much straight away. Concentrate your resources. Get value for your efforts. Select a few areas which account for important sources of strain in your job.

TIME MANAGEMENT...

You have already looked at the different types of overload – quality, quantity and complexity and seen how work study techniques might help improve things.

To go further you need to record all your major activities in your job. This provides you with a list of main categories. It might include such items as:

attending meeting
writing reports
travelling
telephoning
writing letters
interviewing etc.

When you have listed these, prepare a time diary in which you can record how much time you spend on each activity. Break the diary down into fifteen-minute intervals. Select a suitable recording period – not for instance during the annual sales conference. This needs to be at least two weeks. Note what you do during each of these:

9.00 open post
9.15   ''
9.30 management meeting
10.00   ''
10.30   ''
11.00 technical discussion
and so on.

At the end of the recording period, calculate the percentage of time you spend at each, for example:

meetings	30 per cent
writing	22 per cent
telephoning	18 per cent

interviewing	10 per cent
other activities	20 per cent

In this example the 20 per cent for 'other activities' is quite high and you would need to break this down and examine it in more detail.

In a survey of IBM managers, their allocation of time was:

attending meetings	20 per cent
travelling	35 per cent
writing reports	10 per cent
telephoning	6 per cent
letter writing	4 per cent
miscellaneous	25 per cent

Examine your interruptions. One study showed that the average manager was interrupted every eight minutes. This doesn't mean that he or she is regularly interrupted. You may go for two hours before you find that the interruptions are themselves interrupted! Some of us actually encourage interruptions. Every time someone comes into our office with a request, we deal with it straightaway. We are training people to interrupt us. Quite a few managers like to deal with other people's problems because it stops them getting on with their own. Others like the feeling of lots of activity – the more interruptions, the better. We feel that lots of things are happening.

Once you've done this analysis, you can select worthwhile areas to improve your competencies. It is a waste of time improving report writing, if you only write a small report every other year!

You might like to return to the section on work overload in the last chapter and look at how work study techniques could be applied to your job.

Look back over the last month or so and see whether any of your overloads could have been avoided if you thought ahead. What exactly caused problems? Were they all so unexpected?

You need to be clear about the priorities in your job. There are items you have to attend to, others are desirable but not essential. Look at how you allocate your time between these two categories. You also have to be careful that you do not deal with important items when you are tired. You may find that there is a time of the day when you are more creative and another time when you are quite happy to deal with routine matters. If you match your work to your personal profile, you'll get more done.

Don't curse yourself for postponing things. Make a habit of postponing tasks that can be left. As well as a system of priorities of importance, you can develop a system of priorities of urgency. Make a list of what you need to do during the day. Allocate grades 1 – very important, 2 – important and 3 – not so important and A – urgent, B – needs attention, C – could wait. Revise your list and gradings during the day. Work that is A1 must be done but work that is C2 can easily be left if you are pressed for time.

Help others to be brief when they visit you. Summarize what they've said in a few words. Reinforce their behaviour by thanking them when they come straight to the point.

Become more of a proactor – that is acting upon circumstances so that you create the momentum, rather than a reactor who just responds to pressures.

Ask yourself what you could do with another hour a day. Would it really make that much difference? Mentally balance what you would have achieved with that hour and compare it with other tasks you actually got through. Was the hour more important than what you actually did? If it was, you need to look at your priorities.

If your difficulties are caused by other departments, ask to discuss things with them. It is amazing what can happen. I once ran a course for managers, all of whom had time problems connected with other people or other departments. I stopped the course and had everyone visit the departments or people concerned. What was the point of only talking about problems! Not all – but most – managers were able to report constructive solutions to their problems. In some cases, they were not real problems at all. It was just that the other departments did not know what was needed.

Discuss your time problems and how you have tried to tackle them with your boss at your annual appraisal. State that one of your aims is to find a realistic solution to your difficulties at the meeting.

GIVING PRESENTATIONS...

Most managers spend 60 to 70 per cent of their time communicating – in writing, interviewing, attending meetings and giving presentations. One task that produces considerable stress is giving presentations.

Even the thought of having to get up and present ideas is frightening to some of us. Part of the problem is being afraid of being afraid. Some degree of 'nerves' is not only natural but actually helps you deliver a better talk. Being aroused stimulates you and helps you make your talk more exciting. You think more quickly and respond more aptly.

Many speakers become aware that they feel tense. They then become worried about this – and become even more anxious. Now they have to deal with their anxiety *and* give a speech! They find the dual problem too much and become overaroused. 'Nerves' then start to affect their performance negatively.

The problem starts with construing 'nerves' as something negative.

Another aspect is the way the whole situation is construed. Here are some meanings people have built into speaking:

1 'My audience is against me.' Maybe they are, but nearly always, at worst, they are neutral. Generally they feel sympathetic to the speaker. You might have one or two awkward ones occasionally. Even here you do not have to let them dominate you. Just reflect their questions back to them and calmly give your views. If they are persistent ask other members of the audience for their opinions on the points raised, or say something like: 'We disagree there'.

2 'I will fail and make a fool of myself.' 'Failing' often means being afraid of forgetting part of the speech. You will forget something. We all do. No one can remember everything. What you can do, however, is make certain you remember the key points by writing them down. Don't write out the whole speech, just headings of main points. Trust yourself. You have a 'sub-routine' in your memory that will automatically clothe your ideas in suitable words. In normal conversation you do not think out what you are going to say, the words just come tumbling out – all in the right order: subject, verb, object, time, place, location with changes in the normal order to emphasize points. This capacity remains with you when you speak to a group.

The 'inner-game' of public speaking suggests that you have all the capabilities you need. You know how to process incoming reactions from your audience as long as you look at them. You already know how to use appropriate gestures to stress points and how to vary your voice. Let yourself be yourself.

3 'The audience will realize that I don't know what I am talking about.' If in reality, your audience knows more than you, ask yourself why are you speaking to them. They should be speaking to you! What this statement usually means is that perhaps one person may know more. Quite likely sometimes. So what! If you're asked something you don't know, say you don't know. If it is important and no one in the audience can help you out, tell your questioner that you'll find out.

Here are some points which might help you:

1 OBJECTIVES. Be clear about these and ask yourself whether they are possible in the time you have available in relation to the subject you have to present and the existing knowledge, interests and attitude of your audience. Be realistic.

Write out your objectives. Everything you do should be aimed at achieving them.

2 PREPARING. You are already clear about your objectives, now consider these points:

who are your audience
what do they already know about your subject
how interested in it are they
what is in it for them
what likely attitudes do they hold
how strong are these
what barriers may you have to overcome?

Focus strongly on your audience. If your audience has mixed views, select a smaller target audience at whom to direct your main ideas.

If you feel that your ideas will be strongly opposed, a vigorous speech will be counterproductive. Attitudes will harden. You will find a low key speech more effective. Present your audience's ideas first and then gently bring in your own. If you try to push your ideas too powerfully, the result will be a 'boomerang effect', bouncing back at you, leaving the audience feeling even more opposed as they take up ego-defensive positions.

If your audience is already with you, you can present an enthusiastic speech which will carry them even further along your lines.

Establish your main points. These are points you want your audience to remember. Limit them to three or four. Your audience will find it difficult to retain many more. Each point should help you achieve your objective. Link your points with a common theme.

If you have, for example, twelve points to make:

1 2 3 4 5 6 7 8 9 10 11 12

your audience might remember three or four; but if you 'chunk' your information, you'll get this effect:

```
    2       6        10
1 3 4     5 7     8 9 11 12
```

You've linked points 1, 3 and 4 to major point 2 and so on. Your audience is likely to remember much more. You are structuring your material to suit human memory. The hierarchy of points need not stop at two levels. You can develop further with sub-sub-points.

Write your main points out with key ideas next to them, place further development in the third column:

Main points key ideas development
1   1.1   1.1.1

and so on for the rest of the outline. Develop your points in language your audience will easily understand. Back up what you say with facts, information and vivid examples to make them stick. Use words that your audience can mentally visualize. Prefer short words and sentences to long-winded ones. Go directly to the point.

3 PRESENTING YOUR IDEAS. Having your ideas accepted depends upon your credibility. This is based upon whether your audience feels that they can trust you, consider you competent and whether they think they might like you as a person. To look friendly helps! If they don't already know you, the beginning of your talk will help them make up their mind about some of these points.

First impressions count. Say something interesting and powerful when you start. Then preview the way your talk is going to develop. This creates expectations, aids memory and gives the audience an overall structure to hang on to. Build up the talk logically, making sure your audience is aware of the logic by explaining how parts link together. At the end, go over the main points again.

Finally, add a conclusion. Research on attitude change shows that clearly emphasizing conclusions makes a talk more convincing. The only time not to do so, is when the conclusions adversely and personally affect people, that is make them ego-defensive. In this case, simply spell out the main points, leaving the audience to put them together and consider the consequences.

People remember the unusual, so link your ideas to interesting word pictures or visual aids. They get your ideas across. They aid memory. Add interest by engaging more than one sense.

With visual aids, you need:

to present only one main idea or link
to aim for simplicity
to ensure plenty of white space
not to overload with too many words or graphics
to use graphics rather than words
to be bold and clear.

Take a look at advertisements. See how these are laid out. They usually have one eye-catching design and then related text. Computer assisted visual aids make it all easy. You can see your design on screen and when you are satisfied, get it printed on a transparency. You can see figures presented as graphs, pie charts, bar charts etc at the touch of a key.

Colour increases effectiveness. Contrast is best; black on white, white on black, black on yellow and so on. Avoid combinations such as light green on dark green. Use lettering that is easy to read and prefer lower case.

Make use of graphics from illustrations. You can easily reproduce them on modern photocopiers.

Beware of using visual aids to help just you and not your audience.

4 REHEARSING. Don't write your speech out in full. Have a few notes of key words. Then sit down and mentally visualize giving the speech. Like an inner film, imagine your audience responding to what you are saying. See yourself making vivid points. If you are not satisfied, modify and re-run your mental film.

5 PRESENTATION. Place a watch in front of you and note the time you are supposed to finish. Monitor your timing occasionally. Your voice needs to be clear, understandable and varied. Talk to people, look at them, make them feel that they are welcome. Try to make the presentation two-way by responding to their reactions to what you say.

MEETINGS MORE OR LESS...

If you are a manager and you worked through the section on how to use your time more effectively, you almost certainly would have listed meetings as a time waster.

Of course, meetings are useful. They help:

– To inform people about what's happening. It is useful to tell a group about new proposals as they all receive the information at the same time. You can deal with questions and reactions. The key factor here is to check that people have a common interest and *need* to know.

– To discuss issues which are of common interest. Group discussions help change attitudes providing no one person – especially the chairman – dominates the group.

– To do a job of work. This depends upon the type of work. Meetings help when people need to integrate what they are doing with other members of a team. If frequent co-ordination is necessary, where sharing of ideas and common skills is needed, then team work and meetings can be effective. If tasks can be done better individually, bringing people together produces second-rate solutions and wastes time.

– To solve problems – groups generate ideas, but calling a group together may not be as productive as giving each member a separate task to solve independently.

– To make decisions – if the group has the authority, the technical skill and the capacity to work as a team, they will not only make decisions but be committed to those decisions.

Here is a SEVEN POINT GUIDE to more effective meetings:

1 Carry out a survey to see how many meetings are really necessary.

2 Consider holding necessary meetings less frequently.

3 Review membership, consider whether members need to attend the whole of the meeting.

4 Combine a businesslike approach with an informal, relaxed style. This means that there is an agenda, members are expected to be prepared, the meeting starts and finishes on time and that discussion is relevant, logical – not jumping from point to point – but that all feel

free to express opinions, doubts and disagreement. Work through conflict until consensus emerges (and even here not everyone has to pretend to agree for the sake of unanimity).

5 No member should dominate and the chairman should remain impartial. The game is not to guess what the chairman wants and then present his (and more rarely her) views.

6 Members listen, give each other a fair hearing and push for high standards not for an acceptable grey solution so that all can finish by lunch time! Criticism is accepted as being constructive; it is about issues not people.

7 The chairman should summarize from time to time and at the end of each item so that members know exactly where they are, what they have decided and what follow-up has been agreed.

REPORT-WRITING

Another major trouble area is report writing. Very few of us enjoy doing it. We tend to put it off until the last minute and then have a ready-made excuse for not doing it well.

Here are some guidelines to help you. Of course, the only way you'll learn is to do it! Bear some of these points in mind when you next produce one of your reports.

Write only if you have something to say. Ask yourself what your readers expect from your report. This helps you focus on the purpose, what to include and exclude and the amount of detail necessary. It also helps you decide on the sequence in which to present your ideas.

Prepare a brief outline of major points something along the lines of the suggestions for preparing a speech and then let the report develop as you write, making changes as you translate your ideas into

text. Be reader-orientated. If you are stuck, imagine you are talking to your readers. What would you say to them?

With a wide readership of different disciplines and levels, write for the primary readers, that is those who are going to use your work.

Consider your readers present knowledge – this suggests how you can link new material to existing understanding. Ask what barriers you may have to overcome for your ideas to be understood and accepted.

If the report is long – over three or four pages – provide a concise but complete summary at the beginning to give the reader a sense of direction. It also helps your readers to decide whether the whole report needs to be read. Write your summary last of all.

Go directly to the point and write so that your reader can process information easily. Work hard to make complex ideas clear. Prefer the simple to the complex, a word to a phrase, the specific to the vague and general, the vivid to the dull. Stress key points. Be brief about the routine but explain complex ideas.

Aim for variety: highlight important points by placing them first or last in sentences or paragraphs; ask questions, change word order.

Use logic which links related ideas together and works from the readers' – not the writer's – frameworks. Present one main idea in each paragraph, use link sentences and signpost the way ahead. Go from the general to the particular.

Let the layout make the report look attractive so that its appearance invites attention and helps readers find their way around the various sections.

Write quickly then edit for accuracy and finally, once again, for style. If you can master a word processor, you'll find your reports become much speedier to produce.

If you find that you don't know how much to put in and at what depth to present your ideas, ask yourself what your reader would find most helpful. If you are still stuck, you can ring them up and ask!

If you find that you edit, rewrite and edit again, examine what alterations you make. Place them in categories. Note how many alterations under each category and aim to improve your style so that you can eliminate the major categories and save time.

PEOPLE SKILLS

This is a major area. We will look at three aspects:

1 A way of analysing behaviour.
2 Delegation.
3 Becoming more assertive.

A look at TA

One major source of stress at work that you may pinpoint from your grid is your relationships with people. A useful way of analysing such difficulties is through Transactional Analysis (TA). You've already been introduced to some TA ideas when you looked at work overload and the psychological game of 'harried'.

Transactional Analysis is a method of looking at the way people interact with each other which provides you with insights into your own and other people's behaviour.

In Transactional Analysis there are three basic ego states, that is, three ways in which you interact or transact with others.

1 PARENT – these transactions are based upon parental and other authority figures from the past. Words like 'must', 'should', 'ought' figure frequently. This ego state offers us automatic rules about how we should behave.

The Parent ego state has two dimensions: critical and nurturing. Critical Parent tells others (and ourselves) what we should do. It is authoritarian. The Nurturing Parent is kind, caring and loving. It is protective. It is important to realize that neither of these states is bad in itself.

Sometimes we need to be critical when, for example, a child leans out of a top storey window. We must act quickly. There is no time to explain the dangers and we certainly would not want the child to learn from experience! When someone is distressed an immediate sympathetic nurturing approach is appropriate. At such times it does not help to be critical. But 'smother' love, being over kind, looking for people to come to us with their troubles, can stifle growth and produce dependency.

2 ADULT – this is the rational, logical, computer-like analyst in us. It is concerned only with facts, seeking out evidence before making decisions. There are many times when this is appropriate but it does exclude the fun of acting irrationally from time to time and also following your intuition. Solutions can sometimes be found from divergent (as opposed to convergent) thinking, the answer we seek is outside the limits of logic. Thinking creatively provides a 'quantum leap'. The Adult, however, need not clash with creative thinking. The two can work together. Our Adult evaluates creative ideas, rejecting the wilder, less practical ones. Our intuition supplies the ideas in the first place.

3 CHILD – in this ego state we act and talk impulsively or as a 'good' little child has been socialized to respond. There are three sub-divisions of this state: Free Child – open, impulsive and fun loving; Adapted Child which behaves as a good little girl or boy should; finally, the 'Little Professor' which is our intuitive part.

Many of us operate from a preferred state. We are, for example, mostly under the control of our Critical Parent. We live by a series of unwritten rules and expect others to do so. We show this not just by the words we use but by the way we use them. Something that seems friendly in print can be made to sound aggressive when spoken. Think of the ways of uttering 'good morning'.

If someone arrives late, your greetings can clearly express your disapproval. Stress can be caused by attempting (and often failing) to meet demands which have been socialized into us. We follow our Parent dictates. We push ourselves to do what we feel should be done. When we don't succeed, we punish ourselves. Thus we have two problems: 1) our 'failures', 2) pushing ourselves in directions we would rather not go. So even if we succeed, we lack inner satisfaction. Some of us follow these inner rules throughout out lives, doing our duty and denying the self we could have been.

It takes at least two to create a transaction, from a transitory 'hello' to the postman to a deep personal conversation. We initiate and respond to each other from similar or different ego states.

There are three sets of transactions:

1 PARALLEL – for example: Parent to Parent:

First speaker: 'Just look at the way young people behave these days.'

Second speaker: 'You are quite right. Only the other day I was reading...'

Here's another example, this time Adult to Adult:

First speaker: 'Could you tell me the results of the new marketing survey?'

Second speaker: 'Yes, our market share has increased by 3% in the small goods sector.'

Or Child to Child:

Speaker one: 'I'm bored, let's go out for a drink.'

Speaker two: 'Yes, let's leave this work, we can say we were held up by the accounts department, they never check up.'

The transaction can be from Critical Parent to Child:

'You should have produced better work than this, what do you think we pay you for.'

Reply:

'I am sorry. It is all my fault. I never seem to be able to do things right.'

These transactions are parallel and they tend to continue. They are mutually reinforcing. Listen to two people talking about the state of the world and what's wrong with it!

2 CROSSED

Transactions can also be crossed. For example, a transaction initiated by the Adult can be responded to with Critical Parent:

First speaker:

'Can you tell me the results of the marketing survey.'

Reply:

'Get your own damn information.'

This set of transactions can no longer continue about the marketing survey.

3 ULTERIOR

The last category of transaction is called 'ulterior'. This is where the overt message says one thing but the hidden message is different.

First speaker:

'Can you complete the report by 5pm?' (Real message: this is not a request, it is an order and an impossible one at that.)

Second speaker:

'Yes.' (Real message: why do you always give me the impossible which I accept and fail at and we both know it.)

OK and not OK

Many of our transactions fit in with the OK existential position mentioned earlier. It is a way of summing up how we generally relate to others.

You may remember the four positions:

I am not OK, you are OK (everyone seems better than me)

I am OK, you are not OK (I feel superior to others)

I am not OK, You are not OK (it is all hopeless)

I am OK, you are OK (a mentally healthy position)

Most of us are a mixture; we operate more from one position, depending on how we see our current situation. We may be different at work than at home (for example, the tough boss dominated at home by his wife).

Using our time

Another important concept in TA is about the way we structure time. There are six possibilities:

1 WITHDRAWAL – we cut ourselves off from other people. This may or may not be just physical contact. We can be alone in the midst of others. We might even be in the most intimate physical relationship with somebody and yet mentally not be there.

2 RITUALS – these are superficial transactions. For example: 'hello', 'goodbye', 'nice day' and so on.

3 PASTIMES – this is small talk, often used at parties. The talk is about the weather, children, holidays, cars and so on. Next time you are at a party make a list of the pastime subjects talked about.

4 ACTIVITIES – these are shared transactions about getting something done.

5 GAMES – you have already been introduced to one of these. They are transactions which have hidden pay-off, usually negative. The small dialogue about the marketing survey might have been the beginning of a game.

There are many different games. They include:

WOODEN LEG – but for my disability I would pull my weight

NIGYSOB – (now I've got you, you son of a bitch) a way of trapping people

BLEMISH – always finding fault

KICK ME – that was the game of the second participant in the marketing episode. He would end up being blamed and he knew it.

Others include: LUNCH BAG – always working on the job, no time for lunch and HARRIED, which you saw earlier.

Games reinforce our existential position. They remind us of who we are and how we relate to others. They get us strokes, ie recognition from others – even if they are negative. Many of us would rather be criticized than ignored.

In games players take on one of three roles. The roles are swapped as the game proceeds.

The roles are: Persecutor, Victim and Rescuer. Persecutors push and punish others, Victims 'invite' others to put them down and Rescuers try to reduce the suffering. The roles change, as for instance when Persecutors feel guilty, try to rescue their partner and then frequently find the Victim has turned Persecutor and they find themselves now the Victim.

Take a look at business meetings. How much time is spent on each of these activities? Sometimes a lot on rituals and games and little on work itself.

Strokes

Strokes can be conditional: we blame someone for a mistake or praise them because they have done a good job of work. Surveys show that many employees – including senior managers – do not feel that they receive enough positive strokes. A way of getting others to repeat something good which they have done is to reinforce their behaviour by praising them, specifically pointing out what was positive about their efforts.

If you just praise, they feel good but don't quite know what to do next time. There is also a time to be critical but you need to be constructive and deal with the situation rather than the person. You want to help them learn not to go away hating you and the firm.

Unconditional strokes are the other type: you just dislike someone and they know it. There is nothing in particular that they've done. It is just them. Positive unconditional strokes are to let someone know that you appreciate them, like and perhaps love them just because they are who they are. They don't have to *do* anything. Perhaps this is what we all miss sufficiently.

Don't grumble because you don't get enough positive strokes – start giving them!

6 INTIMACY. Is the last way of structuring time. This is open, honest, genuine and real contact between persons.

In some occupations, one of these ways of structuring time may predominate: shopkeepers spend their time in rituals, nuns in withdrawal and a country postman in pastimes. Some of us, because of our jobs, have to spend time alone, for example a shepherd; or in rituals – the doorman at a hotel.

None of these is wrong in itself (except games), but for many of us the balance is not quite right.

Take a look at how you spend your time. If you're dissatisfied, what changes do you want and what could you do to achieve them? Some people keep back from others because they fear their own vulnerability. Perhaps you need to learn to accept this.

Work out how much time you spend on each of these and how it compares with how you'd like it to be.

	Present allocation	Preferred allocation
1 Withdrawal.		
2 Rituals.		
3 Pastimes.		
4 Activities.		
5 Games.		
6 Intimacy.		

Although Transactional Analysis seems simple, it does provide a useful framework for you to examine other people and your behaviour. Unless others understand the concepts it is counter-productive to go around telling them of your analysis of their behaviour!

DELEGATION

Delegation means entrusting to a subordinate, for whom you are responsible, certain clearly defined tasks, authority and responsibility. Authority means the right to use resources within specific limits and responsibility means being liable to be called to account for actions taken. You retain overall responsibility. Delegation does not mean offloading work you don't like just because you don't like it.

Delegation takes time. You need to explain, supervise and let's admit it – it includes some risks. But delegation frees you for more important tasks. It helps motivate people.

To delegate effectively you need to list all your major work areas, consider those which are likely to decline and those which will change in the future. You will also have to think of new tasks which are likely to be allocated to the department in the next year or so. List the tasks you feel suitable for delegating. These are ones that are not your personal responsibility, anything confidential or tasks which require your special skills. You might even start the other way round and ask what tasks you do that *cannot* be delegated.

You need to be clear about what you want done – the end results. You might initially include instructions about how the job is to be done but you are more concerned with results than means.

Next consider the skills, qualities and interests of those who report to you. You also have to take into account your subordinates' present work load. You do not want to overload some, while others have little to do. Match these skills, interests and time available with the tasks you want to delegate.

You can delegate at three levels:
1 Fully.
2 Your subordinate reports on completion.
3 He/she checks with you first before starting.

Which level depends upon existing skills. As subordinates become more skilled, you entrust them with greater responsibility and authority. You let them get on with the job. Initially you may want them to check things out with you first, so that you can ensure that they are on the right lines. Don't just tell them how to do the job – ask them how they can see it being done. If you feel that they don't fully understand, feed back the problems to them, so that they can face the difficulties that their methods might involve.

You need to brief your staff and get them to go away and write down what it is they think you have told them. You can then check that what they have written is a correct interpretation of your briefing and make any necessary amendments. Getting clear instructions at the start is vital.

Initially, you'll need to coach and support them. Remember that people learn at different rates. Some are quick (and might make mistakes). Others are much slower. Let them work at their own pace. After they've learned what to do, let them get on with it but do build in a non-restrictive reporting system. You need the minimum information to tell you that things are not going as they should – management by exception.

As well as this formal monitoring system, you need 'management by conversation'. That is, you informally get the feel of how things are going. If you sense problems, you make it clear that you are there to help. You should be more concerned with problem-solving than with blaming.

Hold regular meetings with your staff so that they can contribute ideas on wider and more strategic issues. Keep them informed about new developments.

This is different from being over-friendly, 'one of the boys', where your main motivation is to be liked. There will be times when you need to be tough and you might have to pass on unpleasant news.

All those working for you will have a variety of tasks and will have different personalities. It is important, therefore, that you are able to use a number of management styles and are flexible enough to change when appropriate.

BECOMING MORE ASSERTIVE

One major problem with managers, employees and most of us, is the inability to say 'no'. Our ever-open-door invites visitors. Always agreeing to help others trains them to ask! Saying 'yes' to all you're asked to do, is an open invitation to others to push work in your direction.

The way out is to become more assertive. Being more assertive can open up new and more constructive ways of dealing with colleagues and others. It helps reduce stress by providing techniques which lead to more control over your life.

The most important point to remember is that assertiveness is different from being aggressive.

You can respond in one of four ways when you are asked to do something you do not want to do:

1 Be passive and accept.
2 Agree but try to wreck things in a hidden way.
3 Fight back openly. You're out to win, someone must lose and it is not going to be you.
4 Be assertive – you acknowledge your rights and those of others.

Mary is asked to work late. She has a date but she finds herself saying 'yes', staying a couple of hours extra and missing her date. Her acceptance reinforces her manager's behaviour. He will be inclined to make similar requests again in the future.

Tom also agrees to stay late but makes certain that some important information is missing and in such a way that his manager will take the blame.

Joe has a big row and storms out of the office.

June says that she knows the project is important but she has a date which she wishes to keep. She offers to help out tomorrow, at lunch-time if necessary. If her boss pushes her, she repeats that she cannot help. She does not say she is sorry, neither does she sound aggressive or confronting. If her manager continues his demands, she continues to repeat her first message.

Being assertive means standing up for your rights and doing so in a non-apologetic manner. Your rights include you making a decision about your free time, the right to present your views and to refuse unfair requests – all without feeling guilty.

To develop assertiveness, you need to use the shaping techniques discussed elsewhere. Begin with slightly threatening situations and when you can comfortably handle them, move on to more difficult areas. If you feel really worried about trying this out in real life, you can use your imagination. Just visualize yourself saying 'no'. As soon as you feel tense, use the relaxation techniques of breathing out slowly as you count: one, two, three, four, five.

Visualization is powerful. Grasp what you need to do and imagine yourself doing it. Daydream of yourself coping, saying the things you want to say.

The actual techniques are straightforward: state what you want and repeat if necessary. Make no excuses. Do not be apologetic.

Let your partner understand that you know what's being asked by reflecting back his request. Then make your statement something like this: 'I understand, Joe, that you want me to work late because the project is important but I have a date and it is impossible for me to stay tonight.'

If you are being criticized and you feel that it is justified, then accept and state that you want to use the session as a problem-solving one.

Limit your assertiveness to issues that are important.

A complementary skill which will help you interact with people more effectively is active listening. The first part of active listening is to pay full attention to your partner. Look as well as listen to them. Note the tone of voice, how they hold themselves, what they do with their hands and look at their faces. People don't communicate only with their voices. They use the whole of their bodies. If you don't look, you miss the complete picture.

Reflect their body posture by sitting as

they do and placing your arms to reflect how they hold theirs. Do not invade their space. This is threatening.

Active listening also includes reflecting what your partner has said. If the statement is long reflect the gist of it, the main points or the last part.

Here is an example:

first person – '...and it is difficult to get the work done, especially when Mary's not there.'

second person – 'I see, especially when Mary's not there?'

first person – 'Yes, that's right...'

Note how the second person, in reflecting, presents her statement (by the tone of voice) as a question. This offers the first person a chance to modify her statement. She could have said:

'Yes but... Mary...not really, it is Fred who is the problem.'

Here's an example reflecting the main points:

'So as I see it, from what you've said, Joe, there appear to be three things bothering you: first the new system, then the extra work-load and finally Mary is away too much?'

In this example the gist is reflected:

'So what you appear to be saying Joe, is that costs are far too high?'

A further method is to reflect your partner's feelings:

'..and that makes you angry?'

A final and more difficult skill is to reflect the underlying message;

'You agree with the scheme, Joe, but the message I get is that you don't have time to deal with people's problems?'

You can add to reflecting techniques, simple comments that indicate you are interested in what is being said. These statements give your partner permission to continue.

Here are some examples:

'Tell me more'

'Oh'

'That sound'

'I see'

'Yes...'

'Go on'

'And...'

If you have t have time for yo from going arou people by thinki to get yourself l .... is also different from the 'ever open door', inviting interruption. You need time to get on with your work undisturbed and your boss and fellow workers need to know this. They also need to know that when you are willing to discuss things, you are an attentive listener.

PROBLEM SOLVING AND DECISION-MAKING...

It helps to have a systematic method to use for solving problems and making decisions.

Here is a FOUR point plan to guide you through more effective decision making.

1 GET TO GRIPS WITH THE ISSUE

Don't act impulsively. Spend time defining the problem. Write it down. Then ask yourself if it really is the problem you first thought it was.

Consider the background and other related problems. Your difficulties could be part of a larger problem. Ask yourself who really 'owns' the problem.

Check your definition. What information is missing? How valid and reliable is the information you have? What do you need to do to get essential information? From whom? When? How?

Look for patterns and possible causes; there is rarely only one.

Centre on objectives rather than difficulties. Where are you now and where e to be? What would be different problem was solved?

down your objectives. Categorize into:

essential

desirable

List benefits, advantages and disadvantages. Move outside the realm of your problem and see how solving it would help or hinder other parts of the organization. Modify your objectives if necessary.

Consider long-term, short-term and immediate needs.

2 MOVING TO A SOLUTION

You need to get the facts, analyse them and develop alternatives that will help you meet your objectives.

A complementary method is brainstorming. Fantasize about the problem, turn it upside-down. Redefine it. Make it more abstract, more concrete. Let your ideas flow, write down every possible – including crazy – way of solving your problem. Use your intuition. Get others to work with you in a 'no holds barred' open meeting where no suggestion is criticized. Evaluate later.

Test tentative solutions before accepting one of them.

If you can't get what you want, what then? What compromise are you willing to accept?

3 MOVING FROM WHERE YOU ARE TO WHERE YOU WANT TO GO

Methods you can use include:

HEURISTICS. This is a rule-of-thumb approach. You start from where you are and consider each possible move towards your goal. You evaluate it by asking how much nearer it would take you to your objective. Try to develop alternative moves.

MEANS-END ANALYSIS. You define your starting state and your desired end state. Decide what you need to bridge the gap. Produce sub-goals, breaking tasks into smaller parts, each with a starting and end state. Break the sub-goals down into even smaller sub-sub-goals. Select means that will move you from the beginning of each goal (sub or sub-sub) to its end. Develop alternative routes.

ANALOGUE/DIGITAL. Not all solutions are 'all or nothing'. Many can be graded with different weights (analogue). It is the correct mixture, made up of different sub-solutions of different weightings, that maximizes your results.

MINI-MAXING. This is useful if you are competing against others. You put yourself in your opponent's shoes and think how he would respond to your move.

It works like this:

your alternative moves
benefit to you (scale of 1–10)

A	B	C	D
5	3	2	6

opponent's possible moves
benefits to him

A1	A2	B1	C1	D1	D2	D3
2	9	2	6	3	1	5

your possible moves
and so on

For the first move, you have four alternatives. Each provides benefits. Move A provides you (or so you think) with five points of benefit but your opponent could counteract with A2 and gain nine points to your disadvantage. Move D on your part gives you six points and, as far as you can see, your opponent by counteracting with move D3, would gain only five points.

You need to go to a few further stages, thinking out possible moves for each eventuality and the benefits and counter-benefits.

This method stops you making initially

beneficial moves which can later turn out to the advantage of your opponent.

Four stages are likely to be the maximum you could handle. The number of possibilities for yourself and your opponent become too many and there is an horizon effect which could wipe out your last best benefit. You reach the limit and cannot think of the very large number of counter-moves beyond the horizon.

4 THE LAST STAGE

Once you've decided where you want to go and how you are going to get there, you still have the most important part of the whole process to do!

You have to do four things:

1 Sell it to others.

2 Build in a control system to see how things are progressing.

3 Create contingency plans for what is likely to go wrong.

4 Review – see how things turned out and how your decision making could have been improved!

The suggestions in this section help you to become more proficient as a manager. This, in itself, reduces stress in your work-life. If they are used as a follow-up to a detailed analysis which pinpoints your own specific problems and you have learned to relax, you will find that you control your work-life, rather than feeling it controls you.

TOPIC REFERENCES

Transactional Analysis:

Berne, Eric., *Transactional Analysis in psychotherapy'*, Condor, 1961.

James, M. and Savory, L., *A new self – self therapy with Transactional Analysis*, Addison-Wesley, 1977.

Jongeward, D. and Seyer, P., *Choosing success*, Wiley, 1978.

Steiner, C., *Scripts people live by*, Grove Press, 1974.

CHAPTER 11

Finally...

If you have read this book and worked through some of the exercises, you will now know more about yourself and what stresses you.

You may begin to see things differently. Sometimes when we are stressed, it is impossible to see the opposite pole:

stressed ⟵——————⟶ ?

We don't know what it is like to be unstressed. It is almost as if it has no meaning for us. Stress is so much part of our lives. We may feel that stress tells us that we are pulling our weight.

Gradually we begin to see that life need not be like that. It is not that previous perceptions were wrong, but as if we were blind and now we see shape and colour for the first time. All that we sensed previously was correct. It hasn't changed at all. What is different is the way we see things now.

Alternative ways of seeing things is a key idea behind this book. You need not be imprisoned. You can liberate yourself and open up more possibilities than you ever thought could enter your life.

Another important concept is to take responsibility for yourself. This is tough, difficult and sometimes you feel you get nowhere. But it is eventually liberating. You realize that you have the capacity to take charge of your life. You don't sit back and take out what is handed to you.

An important stress buffer which has emerged from research is 'hardiness'.

This consists of:

believing you can *control* things

being *committed* to what you want out of life, to your family, your job, and society

seeing *challenge* as an opportunity to develop yourself

See how you can build these qualities into your life.

If you feel you need professional help, then seek it but still remain in control of yourself.

Start from where you are. Move in small steps. Test things out. Just reducing stress a bit proves that you do have power over your life.

Important too, is that you learn to relax and practise daily, so that gradually you shed the tensions built up over the years.

Use visualization to see yourself coping, being positive, concentrating on solutions not problems and doing what you want to do. Don't clutter your mind with negative, defeatist thoughts – let your daydreams be filled with hope.

Perseverence is necessary. Do not expect everything to change by just dabbling with a few grids and one or two attempts at relaxation.

Attempt things – even if you are afraid. Don't wait until you are confident before you try. Confidence comes from doing such things despite your fears.

See what you do as an experiment. Whether it works or doesn't you still gain. It is a pathway to competence.

You do not have to be the victim of your physical disposition, your childhood, your class or present circumstances. You can be the creator – of yourself.

TOPIC REFERENCES

Kobasa, S., *Hardiness and Health*, Journal of Personality and Social Psychology 42, 1982.

Useful addresses

For details of counselling in the UK:

British Association of Counselling
37a Sheep Street
Rugby
Warwickshire CV21 3BX (0788) 78328–9

For courses in Personal Construct
Psychology:

Centre for Personal Construct
Psychology
132 Warwick Way
London SW1V 4JD (01) 834 8875

For in-company stress reduction
courses, individual stress counselling,
related problems and computer repertory grid analyses:

KAPA Consultancy
9 Mottingham Gardens
London SE9 4RL (01) 857 7391

Other addresses:
British Society for Experimental &
Clinical Hypnosis
Dr M Heap
Department of Psychology
Middlewood Hospital
Sheffield S6 1TP

American Psychological Association
1200 Seventeenth Street NW
Washington DC 20036
USA

Australian Society for Clinical & Ex-
perimental Hypnosis
Royal Melbourne Hospital
Royal Parade
Parkville
Victoria
Australia

To accompany this book, a relaxation
cassette is available from booksellers or
the publishers.

Further reading

Bannister, D. and Fransella, F., *Inquiring man: the theory of personal constructs* Penguin, 1971.

Beail, N., *Repertory grid techniques and personal constructs*, Croom Helm, 1985.

Fransella, F. and Bannister D., *A manual for repertory grid techniques*, Academic Press, 1977.

Wilson, K. and Hunt, E., *How to survive the 9 to 5*, Thames/Methuen, 1986.

Wood, C., *Living in overdrive*, Fontana, 1984.

Index

Other recommended reading ...

YOUR COMPLETE STRESS PROOFING PROGRAMME

How to Protect Yourself Against the Ill–Effects of Stress

Leon Chaitow, N.D., D.O, M.B.N.O.A.

"Don't work so hard – you'll kill yourself!" And its true. Overwork – stress – can, and does, kill! We've all heard of businessman's ulcer – this is a stress-related disease. Heart attacks, arthritis, eczema – all are stress-related diseases. You may not be able to relieve the pressure but your body can – and will if properly trained – cope with it much better. This book by Leon Chaitow will teach you not only how to cope with, but actually overcome, stressful situations. Includes! Diet and nutrition; rythmic abdominal breathing; progressive muscular relaxation; water treatments; full spectrum lighting:- biofeedback; concentrative meditation; colour visualization, and guided imagery for self-healing.

FIT TO MANAGE

An Executive Fitness Guide to Peak Performance

Graham Jones

Modern business life is a hurried and aggressive affair – a fierce competitive world where positive results are demanded, and demanded now, if not sooner! Each day is busier that the last with little evidence of a 'light at the end of the tunnel', but with a very real threat of redundancy, or worse, being 'squeezed out' hanging over every day.

The potential rewards are great – a nice home, an expensive car and a happy and financially secure retirement. But the potential hazards are even greater – you may never live to reach retirement!

* 60 million working days each year are lost through heart disease or circulatory disorders. 1 in 4 people in the UK die of heart disease.

* 58 million working days each year are lost due to muscle and bone disorders – the results of life behind a desk.

* 50 million working days each year are lost because of mental disorders due in part to high-stress lifestyles.

These are average figures. Hard driving go-getters face increased risks. The ambitious, competitive excutive is just the sort of person who will suffer a heart attack and die before being able to reap the rewards of a promising career.

Many of the conditions from which they die could have been prevented.

Fit To Manage pin-points problem areas and offers a plan of action that will enable you to proof yourself against the consequences of 'cut-and-thrust' business life, to radically reduce the risk of ill-health...to survive long enough to enjoy your hard-earned retirement!

It fills the gap between business books and keep-fit books, tackling the specialist requirements of business men and women who need to keep fit despite the pressure of their lifestyles.